Faint Heart Never Kissed a Pig

Faint Heart Never Kissed a Pig

Ann Drysdale

Routledge & Kegan Paul
London and Henley

First published in 1982 by Routledge & Kegan Paul Ltd
39 Store Street, London WC1E 7DD and Broadway House, Newtown Road,
Henley-on-Thames, Oxon RG9 1EN
Set in 11 on 13pt Garamond by
Rowland Phototypesetting, Bury St Edmunds, Suffolk
and printed in Great Britain by
St Edmundsbury Press, Bury St Edmunds, Suffolk

British Library Cataloguing in Publication Data

Drysdale, Ann

Faint heart never kissed a pig.
1. Country life – England – Yorkshire
2. Yorkshire (England) – Social life and customs
I. Title
942.8′1′085   DA670.Y6

ISBN 0-7100-0972-0

Contents

Introduction

Hagg House was about a quarter of a mile from the road, down a drive. It was towards the end of October, but the sun was shining and there was warmth in it. My elder son Andrew's hair glowed an incredible shade of red as he got out of the car to open the gate. It was like a beacon that led us into the yard as he ran ahead of us, and we joined him outside the door, and looked up.

We saw an amazingly angular house of grey stone, like a hollow brick standing on its edge. It was adrift on a raft of concrete amid a tangle of seeding nettles and fading bracken. An orchard full of an awesome abundance of small, black plums. Three small sheds, each with its own little yard, awaiting occupation. The whole place was waiting. It sat halfway down a gentle valley, looking, as its lucky occupants would look, down a green field, over a noisy river, and up again, to a huge purple hill whose colours had run together into an amalgam of honey and wine that you could almost taste. We stood in the patch of sunlight and looked. To the left a beechwood above the river, to the right little empty homesteads on the side of the hill, waiting to be explored. Above, a tangled meadow, with a stream that hastened through a hazel copse and detoured thoughtfully to linger in the garden before it went its inevitable way to the river. And all around were curious eyes. Rabbits, poised for flight.

Pheasants, with happy memories of the gamekeeper who had lived there before, who didn't see any reason to draw back. Cattle, who left their serious search for the last dregs of goodness in the autumn grass to gather at the fence and stare without malice. One or two sheep enjoying their last weeks of aimlessness before their time was taken up entirely with the business of ensuring their annual pregnancy. So much gentleness, and over it all the smell of woodsmoke, the very essence of autumn.

Autumn has always been, for me, more of a promise than spring. A Londoner's upbringing has made it special. Autumn was coming home from work one day and realising that something had changed, for autumn comes swiftly to the cities, without the conscious period of change that the countryman has time to savour. So suddenly would it come that at first I would mistake it for winter, and it was something pleasant to recognise it for what it was, and to realise that there was yet, still, a little time. In London, autumn was the most poignant, the most evocative, mood of the year, and with that first realisation of its coming, the memories, all of them bound up with autumn, would come flooding back. My fashionable shoes would prod with skinny heels at the leaves lying under the horse-chestnut tree on the corner of the street where I used to live, and I would remember myself, in the sensible, laced-up shoes of a schoolgirl, and it would seem then that all my life had been made up of a succession of autumns. I would step from leaf to leaf, convinced that if I had, by some misfortune, some natural displacement of the leaf-carpet on the pavement, to tread on the stone, some terrible misfortune would await me when I got home. It was on that corner, under the horse-chestnut tree where I changed, quite consciously, from my school self to my home self. I remembered myself coming along, with my satchel on one shoulder, incredibly heavy, because I felt compelled to carry all my most prized possessions about with me rather than leave them behind, walking with my head bent forward, never running that last stretch as I did the rest of the way, watching my feet in the laced-up shoes and feeling loneliness, and the strange exultation in it, that I have felt so often since, and been unable to put a name to.

But here I was, in autumn, and the too-bright sunshine and the smoke smell of it were still the same. This new autumn did not look forward to winter and chilblains and lighted buses in the sudden dark, but back, lazily, over the summer memories that the London autumns blotted out with the first yellow fog. There again, as I stood there, were all the summers of that same child. The sandals without socks. My grandmother's little cottage with the oil-lamps and bed-at-nine, after the news. There was the smell of tractor fuel heavy in the air, and the tiredness of the long days. Dustmotes in the threshing-barn, and barley whiskers against the skin. Stubble scratches on which the blood had dried in grubby specks. The acclamation of the farm-workers when the little townie found the lost nest or rode the fearsome Boxer bareback into Sturmer. The cherished waves from the young man who drove the combine, whose handsome face and bronzed back seemed to promise to show me what love was all about, and his elder brother, quiet and gentle, who would truly have shown me if only there had been time before the autumn took me away again. And I knew that this was the root of the dream. That I wanted to give my children all the summers and none of the autumns, and I knew with certainty that this was the place. The house knew too. Hagg House. I would fumble about here and play at country life and no matter what abuses I put it to, this house would know that I meant well. It was a feeling I dared not express aloud because I knew it was fanciful, and that I was engaged on serious business, but it didn't need saying. It was time to go now. Time to write to the owner and discuss rent.

The following Wednesday I was to meet the owner of Hagg House. On the Monday I joked about it. On the Tuesday I sought advice. But on the Wednesday morning I went tentatively to the back door of the lady next door and asked if I might have the loan of one or two matching teaspoons. I had decided that the ancient mugs with scenes of the Crimea and bunny-rabbits at play would lend an air of informality and possibly provide a useful conversation piece, but the spoons I had were decidedly better kept for serving the tinned dogfood with which they had been given away. It was not that I had never possessed any passable cutlery; this state of affairs had been brought about by the fine summer the previous year.

The old Edward where we used to live, you see, was a narrow-boat moored on the Birmingham–Worcester canal, which was used to a greater extent than many others for pleasure traffic. Above our mooring was a flight of thirty locks, and the fine weather had brought them a good deal more traffic than they had been used to. The effects of a single boat's passage up or down the flight was marked by a small tidal wave that was felt quite clearly even some distance away. The effect of this unaccustomed movement, combined with the unusually high number of passing craft, had the effect of deepening the central channel, and silting up the sides, with the result that poor old Edward had settled, by the end of June, on her private mudflat, which was something of a misnomer as it was far from flat. The stern end was very much lower in the water than the bow – perhaps due to the weight of the huge Scammel marine engine that had been fitted in defiance of the speed limit on inland waterways, with the further result that not only was progress forward an uphill struggle, but also the sink, a slave to gravity, would not drain completely unless we had a large party of visitors in the front end to level it up. So I threw my washing-up water straight out of the window. Anyone who has ever cleared up after a meal will know that at the bottom of the bowl there always lurks a breakaway group of hitherto invisible cutlery, but without the use of my sink there was no failsafe device to ensure its being found before it was too late. In my years as a water-gipsy I never made the acquaintance of Davy Jones, but I can say with some conviction that he sets a pretty table. He has all the equipment, one way and another.

So there I sat, with a Lord expected for tea, scouring the stains from the old mugs and setting out my borrowed spoons. I hoped he did not like his tea too strong, as there was a hole in the teapot, just below the spout, and once it was filled, it was a race to pour it before it ran away. Only one other thing could be done to create the impression of impoverished gentility I was striving for, and I did it. May God forgive me, I hid Andrew and the twins, Robert and Nancy, in the kitchen with a packet of chocolate biscuits.

The meeting went as well as I would have expected had I only dared to believe that the man himself could be as pleasant as his letters. But there had still been no final decision when he asked if he might meet the little ones. I loosed them on him like young lions upon a Christian martyr. They were indescribably filthy. Two ten-months babies can make a chocolate biscuit cover a remarkable area, even when it is only half-coated. The twins had excelled themselves and Andrew seemed to have gone one better. I saw the imminent contact between Robert and his Lordship's fine tweed trouser-leg and yelled an agonised warning, but it was brushed cheerfully aside. Within the next few minutes a rent lower than I had dared hope was finalised, and I was left alone with the dream still intact, its edges beginning to harden like the chocolate on Robert's face. I looked at him. His eyes were very bright and very blue. His pinched look was beginning to go.

The move into Hagg House was accomplished slowly and untidily in and atop an elderly Volkswagen. It must have been very picturesque, but I was not able to appreciate it as I always seemed to be travelling under something large and unstable, with an inordinate number of corners. There was a good deal of clearing-up to be done. I found out where flies go in the winter as I swept them up in shovelfuls and piled them up outside. I think most of them came back, but I felt that a token gesture had been made, so I ceased hostilities and concentrated on distributing the furniture as fairly as I could among the empty rooms. What had seemed a huge amount dwindled in the increased space.

On 15 November we moved in. We brought the dog, and the cooker with the cat shut inside, and spent our first night amid a pile of unsorted treasure.

There was a wind that night, and a limpid moon that seemed at odds with it. There was a howling outside the uncurtained windows that brought the moor very near. Things called to one another in the beechwood. I went out into the yard and stood for a long time and felt neither alone nor afraid of my unseen company. The maniac laughter of a grouse whose rest had been disturbed started a chain reaction of unease that rippled down the hill from the moor above the road but there was no malice in it. When I went back into the house I didn't lock the door.

Beginnings

Despite all the warnings we had had, that first winter held little to alarm us. There was Christmas caught up in it somewhere, and a New Year in Scotland which somehow swallowed up the twins' first birthday in the preparations for it. Some time during those months the twins took their first tottering steps, Robert leading and Nancy stumbling after, out over the storm sill into the yard.

They still slept a good deal of the day, and Andrew and I took advantage of those hours to explore the hinterland of Hagg House. We began with the string of outbuildings that stretched on where the house left off, and found mouseholes and swallows' nests, and a press for making counterfeit money that turned out to have no more exciting a function than chopping turnips. There were our own little sheds, empty and waiting, and we would sit in them eating cake and promising ourselves that we would find occupants for them when spring came. And we followed the river paths, and found a poor hill ewe, twisted inextricably in a briar patch. We ran home for the dress-making shears and hacked her free, only to find that she could no longer stand and was sliding helplessly into the river. We had to drag the poor creature to a place of safety while we ran to fetch her owner. And there was the old lime-kiln which made a secret place to hide and watch the heron on the river.

But most of all, we talked to each other. This was the last year before he began school, and I knew that when he did there would be a whole new set of needs and values, that gradually he would build his own dream, probably, I imagined, of city life and excitement, and since I had carried for so long the ache in my heart for the countryside and what I could make it mean to me, I would understand. Even before I had begun, I could see the possible end of it, and I determined that even if I had to wait much longer before I could think of any of it as forever, I would snatch at this chance to show them what it could be like to live my way, with time to teach and space to learn. And I began to long for the spring.

It was not too slow in coming, that year. By March the grass had begun to revive and I began to look in the local paper for a likely goat. We bought straw, and cleaned out the shed for when Emily came, for she was Emily, wherever she was, and we were waiting for her. I had treasured the Blackberry Farm books as a child, and to me all goats were Emilies unless proved otherwise.

I found her on a smallholding not far from Northallerton. A bald-eared, knock-kneed creature the colour of cold tea with a dark brown cross on her back like a donkey, which she bore as though it were fashioned from solid elm, so long-suffering was her appearance. She seemed to have no udder at all — one had to peer underneath to see it as though searching for body-rot on a motor car. She was lopsidedly pregnant with her first cargo of young, due, I was assured, at the end of April. I obtained books from the mobile library on the parturition of goats and studied diagrams of possible malpresentations until I had memorised the differences between difficult and impossible deliveries, and I waited.

The end of April came and went. Emily's forthcoming confinement became first an object of great excitement, then of apprehension and finally, as May wore on, a source of great embarrassment. I felt humiliated, almost as though it were a pregnancy of my own that had failed to come to fruition.

Then, suddenly, on May 25, there were Muriel and Jim.

I had by this time ceased to believe in the creature's fecundity, and it was only the single sharp cry that summoned me to the shed where she stood licking the two mewling bundles as though they were some sort of confection, to be savoured and sucked. It is a strange action, this licking of the newborn. It is not a caressing with the tongue, but more of the energetic action of an urchin on an ice-lolly. Emily's tongue, teeth and rubbery lips were all employed in the ritual cleaning of her young ones and there was a frenzy, an urgency about the action that was not at all gentle. When I bent low to congratulate her she turned and licked my face and hair in the same strange, compulsive way and it was pleasant, but painful, and I had to pull away. I could feel how easy it must be for those smaller animal mothers, particularly of the rodent kind, to devour their young quite unintentionally in this frenetic maternal zeal.

Emily blossomed. Her coat grew sleek and she developed a passable udder. I was grateful, though, for the books that told me that the young should be allowed to suckle unrestricted for the first few days, as it had suddenly begun to give me a sinking feeling when I thought about milking. That, after all, was the reason I had bought her and I was in some doubt as to whether she and I could come to some workable arrangement as to how it should be done. My fears were justified.

Unfortunately, though, I had to keep them to myself. Had I had any good advice or cheerful encouragement I should have been shamed into giving up entirely. After all, I had been the one to broadcast this idea as the most economical and hygienic way of providing milk for the children and quite a few smiles had been politely stifled at the outset, so how could I confess now that, though I still saw the idea as a sound one, the mechanics of the thing had got me beaten?

I had milked cows before, but those were elderly ladies well used to the process. Moreover their calves had long since been taken away and they looked forward to the relief of milking like a human mother who has popped out for half an hour and got caught in a traffic jam. They had huge teats, too. Handsized. To touch them was to send great jets of milk frothing into the pail. But Emily was different.

To look at her you would see only a domestic beast like any other, with a leg at each corner and a perfectly distinguishable front and rear, but when I attempted milking, she grew legs everywhere and bucked and leaped so that one minute my face was pressed into her flank and the next I was looking into her inscrutable amber eyes which had merged into one in the middle of her head because of the proximity of our noses. After the first few tries I decided not to bother to catch any of what came out, as any vessel placed on the ground would end up being worn on her hind feet like a wellington boot, and I simply experimented until I found a way to immobilise everything lethal and still leave myself room to manoeuvre.

The ideas that did not work would sound like author's addenda to the Kama Sutra were I to catalogue them, and are probably best forgotten, especially since most of them ended with Emily disappearing into the hinterland at an impressive rate of knots and myself too exhausted to care whether she ever came back.

The final solution was to tie her collar tightly to the wire mesh of her enclosure, rather high so that only the tips of her toes touched the ground, then grind my left shoulder into the hollow of her flank and reach round between her front and back legs with my left arm, trapping her offside hind leg in the crook of it and using the fingers to press on the hamstring muscle of the nearer one. This left me only the fingers of my right hand to milk with, and since her teats were so small, the action resembled the pill-rolling motions of an advanced case of Parkinson's Disease. But it worked.

At length I had only to speak encouragingly and wave the bucket for her to stand still wherever she was, and yield her milk without the need for any kind of restraint, but on that first wonderful day when I had caught and trussed Emily and secured her in my specialised rugby tackle, and when the first grudging spurts of milk actually landed in the red plastic seaside bucket that I had got from Woolworths, I felt like Alexander sacking Persepolis.

It was on this day that my next-door neighbour passed by on the way to inspect his cattle. 'Hello,' he said. 'Do you know you're milking from the wrong side?' My reply doesn't bear setting down.

Once bitten, twice shy, they say. During my first attempt at keeping ducks I was bitten not once but several times, and the memory is green, and yet I am still wakened as in those days by the unsynchronised soundtrack of a Disney cartoon and the relentless flap of cold, wet feet in the yard.

Not long after Emily moved in, friends of friends foisted upon me four Aylesbury ducks which had been forced to take up residence in their coal-cellar owing to their neighbours' opposition. By the end of the affair I was totally in sympathy with those neighbours, but at the outset I was delighted with the newcomers.

There were two of each sex, the ducks squat and soft with blotchy beaks and headfeathers always a little awry. The drakes stood tall, making virgin ski-slopes from their heads to their tails, where the humorous curled feathers spoiled the symmetry.

All white and yellow and moving in purposeful convoy, they stepped straight from childhood picture-books. They were idealised D-for-ducks, and responded with vulgar haste to the cry of 'Duck, duck' at feeding time. It was not until later that their characters earned them the names of Trixie, Dulcie, Randy and Lonely, and even then these were seldom used.

I was told that they were on the point of a period of productivity, that at any moment they would lay a multitude of huge eggs, that they had been waiting only for the right place to begin their natural activities. But their whole lives seemed to be taken up with less social behaviour. They dibbled in cow-pats with obscene pleasure. They bathed in the mud in the cows' footprints and washed it all off exaggeratedly in the pool where the stream gathers strength before slipping down the culvert under the yard.

They went for long walks in single file, almost unbelievable distances. One would come across them in hollows in the far meadows and they would tip their metaphorical hats and go about their untidy business with studied unconcern, and all the while no sign of an egg. Then they moulted, copiously, in snowy flurries, all over everything.

Our neighbourhood lambs were coming to terms with adolescence and summer was well past its best when those ducks finally cottoned on to what the bees and I had been trying to tell them, and with a shameless disregard of casual observers, embarked upon an outburst of intensive reproduction.

By this time, however, they had become a local joke, and when I found the first eggs, placed centrally in two straw-filled motor tyres, I was so convinced that one of my neighbours must have planted them that I made an extravagant sponge-cake and said nothing. But after a few mornings of sceptical observation it became apparent that the witless creatures had indeed seen fit to justify their pampered existence in the proper manner.

I looked at eggs as though for the first time. How smooth and white, how extra-large, how vulnerable, how eggy they were. The ducks, however, seemed totally indifferent to them. I gathered together a few under a broody hen, with a most notable lack of success. I tried a home-made incubator which produced, from a total of thirty eggs, one premature duckling which survived just long enough to be given a name – Earlybird – and a funeral.

Then they moulted again. About this time the old stone

culvert under the yard became blocked and the estate manager hinted that the ducks might be the cause of the torrent which cut off all but welly-booted approaches to the house. I defended them stoutly, but have always nursed a sneaking suspicion that they had managed it somehow, just out of spite.

For spiteful indeed they were. The children grew afraid to come out into the yard. The ducks pushed open the door and attacked them in the kitchen. They made picnicking impossible and cleaning floors a nightmare. So when a lady called to buy one of my young goats and fell for the sycophantic expression in their evil beady eyes I agreed to sell them with an alacrity that must have betrayed my relief.

But I did it again a year or two later, falling for two little Campbells who were being bullied by their siblings. They seemed quite biddable and pleasant, but one never knows. I put it about that I had engaged them to forage for liver-fluke snails, and peered daily into their bilberry eyes for signs of the territorial chauvinism that I had learned to associate with their kind. I had made up my mind that, if I should be bitten a second time, I should be ready for them. So I called them Sage and Onion.

For one thing, though, I must confess myself grateful to those first dreadful ducks. Without them I would never have met one of the most memorable characters to enrich those early days; nor would I have written my hunting song.

> I like the hunting of the Snark
> Better than that of the hen
> For the squawking sneak with the battling beak
> Strikes fear in the hearts of men . . .

I called it 'The Very New Squire' and it owed a great deal to Wilfred Scawen Blunt, but marginally more to Mrs McGurk, who taught me a great deal about poultry, and not a little about the joys of the chase.

I engaged her as a warm-nurse to that first sitting of foundling duck eggs, and she was the first hen with whom I had ever come into anything like intimate contact. She was dragged shrieking from her own infertile clutch and I took her home in a box, battened down with baler band. But not before I had caught the full force of the malevolence in that terrible eye.

I had borrowed a coop with a wire run, and placed in it, on a nest of straw, four duck eggs. I stuffed the protesting bird on top of them and shut the trapdoor. She settled her scrawny breast on the cold eggs, but her eyes never left my face, and I knew that she knew that she had been deceived. And she knew that I knew that she knew. It was war.

She refused to come out of the coop to eat so much as a crumb for 24 hours. I did not know that this was normal behaviour in a broody bird. I had concentrated my excessive study on the eggs themselves – how they must be aired and watered and turned. I tried appeasement. She drew first blood.

I spoke gently. 'Come on, Mrs McGurk and eat your nice pellets.' I spoke harshly. 'Come out, damn you, you'll starve.' The look in her eyes was pure hatred and I felt belittled. Surely she could tell that I was a kindly soul, that the food I offered was a token of affection, of concern for her welfare. Unlovely thing that she was, if she should die like a sparrow on a winter's night, it would be because I had failed. I had to persuade her that I loved her. I had to demonstrate human omniscience to that steady gaze of acid amber. So I got a stick and poked her. She moved off the nest but withdrew to the dark recesses of the coop. I took the trapdoor off the top of the run, lay prone and fished inside with a gloved hand. She retreated further into the darkness.

I slewed around, leaving more and more of the trapdoor uncovered as I groped for a fistful of feathers. She pecked again, betraying her position, and I made a now-or-never lunge that proved to be never as she countered with a forward rush and a simultaneous leap for the trapdoor. Her strategy was faultless. She was free.

The rush of mixed emotions to my head was delicately countered by the sick sense of loss in the pit of my stomach. I stalked her. She dodged. I tried to drive her back to the nest she had been so reluctant to leave, but she scorned it.

There was an erratic quality in my tactics because of my growing realisation that her hatred for me was stronger than her regard for her foster-eggs, and she took wicked advantage of it. Never once was she out of sight but night came and I was henless still.

I was told that foxes don't eat broodies, that she would survive quite well on her own. When I asked how I should go about recapturing her, I was told 'Grab her' with ill-concealed amusement. The hunt was on.

After a week or so, when the feeling of loss had subsided, it all became fun. People asked after her as though she were an ailing relative and my circle of acquaintances widened considerably. I developed an advanced McGurk-hunting kit consisting of an old raincoat to throw over her and a forked stick to pin her to the ground, a jar of layers' pellets as a lure for the quarry and a quarter of peardrops as solace for the hunter. Every evening she came out to feed and every evening I set out determined and returned defeated.

There were some near misses. Once I came upon her digging in an anthill and she ran off down the footpath to the river, her legs invisible with the speed of her departure, for all the world like a tiny trials rider on a juddering motorcycle. Once I spied her among some bracken and I swear I held her for a breath's length before she slipped from my grasp like so much wet soap and was gone.

Mrs McGurk was teaching me a lot. She showed me that poultry are not always the witless creatures they are put about to be; that there are among them individuals of rounded character just as in any domestic species. She opened the door to the farming community around us. She turned my inflated ideas about poultry-rearing upside-down, and as they waggled their scaly legs in the air, I laughed louder at myself than I had ever had the courage to do before.

But still there was a touch of anger at being thwarted, a lurking fear of predators in the night and the sadness that the very sight, the mere sound of my presence could put a living creature to flight with the desperation of a man running from the gallows. There was no chance now of winning her confidence and with it her love. Brute force it had to be.

One night, at dusk, I walked along the bridle path and spotted her gazing at me from a small rowan tree. I wished that someone had told me that hens roosted in trees. I wondered how many times she had watched me from some point of vantage as I beat the undergrowth, and my teeth gritted.

Mrs McGurk it was indeed, but that month of freedom had changed her from an oven-ready old boiler into a veritable queen of hens. The setting sun glanced off her golden breast and her comb was scarlet on her sooty head. Those terrible eyes were the only remaining link with what I had lost, and now they held a touch of scorn.

I lunged, and she fled squawking for a clump of hawthorns and hid right in the clawing, tearing heart of it. I prodded her out with my stick and she made for a nearby wood, but it was surrounded with rabbit net and she left the jump too late. She veered uphill and disappeared into a clump of bracken by a drystone wall. And there I caught her, her head rammed tight into a crack between the stones and the evening breeze ruffling the downy feathers on her protruding bum. I carried her home, but I sang quietly to her as we went, and there was no triumph in it.

I took her to the tiny shed at the end of our row of buildings. Only the piece of old timber that I had found there, with the neat round hole, its edges carefully chamfered to prevent damage to the human fundament, betrayed its former purpose. There I left her, and the following day I bought four more old hens as ladies-in-waiting for my queen, and they began to lay. Thus it was that a poultry unit was added to an already flourishing dairy enterprise.

It grew, of course, in the same haphazard manner as everything else. A surprising number of people began to use our house as a clearing station. Here I stand, like the Statue of Liberty, offering a safe haven for the overspill of other people's teeming back gardens, and this has furnished many of our most interesting companions. Owl, the bantam with so many extra toes that she appeared to be walking on specially adapted spiders, the Campbell ducks, Ernest Pig, all these and many others came in such circumstances, tempest-tossed, to me. Thus I should have been able to face the episode of the visiting vulture with relative equanimity, but, as it was, it proved a somewhat mind-bending experience.

In the fairly small hours of a Sunday morning I made my wellied way along the side of the sheep-pens to look for a sharpening stone that I had poked into the wall.

The overnight frost crunched in the silence I had created by foddering the complaining livestock, and as I crossed the muddy pen my footsteps sucked and plopped in tune with the heavy feeling of having just got up and gone outside before the kettle boiled.

Not a drop, therefore, of anything had passed my lips and my head was as clear as it is possible for a head to be in such circumstances. So it was something of a shock, you will understand, when I turned back across the pen to see a small, dejected vulture, sitting on the top rail, regarding me with a dispirited air.

I was too surprised to speak to it, so it initiated the conversation with a sound like the swinging of a rusty gate. At the risk of appearing brusque, I returned swiftly to the house and drank two cups of coffee. When I looked again it was still there. Without moving its body, it swivelled its scraggy neck and the beady eyes in the bald, cyanosed head regarded me expectantly.

It occurred to me that the apparition must be concerned in some way with the visit, after dark the previous night, of a friend who had left a consignment of aged hens and unwanted bantams. I had had a hard day, catching sheep for the annual dodding-out ceremony — removal of some of the wool on the tails of the moor sheep before turning the tups among them — and when this latest influx of refugees took place, I merely offered a half-hearted hand to tip the contents of a couple of sacks into the inky interior of the henhouse. I now recalled my friend's mentioning that there was, among my feathered acquisitions, a guinea fowl.

I had imagined this to be some magical amalgam of pheasant and peacock, decorative and delightful. I had imagined some snow-white beauty, longtailed and jewel-crested, strutting proudly among the common hens, whistling — perhaps even singing the odd stave. I had looked forward to daylight.

But there was no doubt about it. This creaking creature splurged on the rails was my dream bird, take it or leave it.

I stared for a long time at its extraordinary face. It sported a little red helmet like a keystone cop, two earholes filled with bristly ginger hairs, the most unlikely pair of curling eyelashes adorning its scaly blue head, and two scarlet wattles quivered below its beak like matronly chins.

It was dumping forlornly along, its navy-and-white, houndstooth checked body humped in an attitude of utter misery, when my elder son vaulted the gate in the downhill rush to his tea. 'Mum!' he shouted, 'the Martians have landed!' He was joined by my younger son who has a profound interest in palaeontology. He asked, 'Where did the Archaeopteryx come from?' My daugher decided the issue. 'It's a Dodo.'

So Dodo he, or she, remained. I asked the person most likely to know how one decided this delicate issue in the case of guinea fowl. The cocks, she told me, have more red on their heads.

I watched it from the window, wending its solitary way along the wheelruts, piping inconsolably to anyone who would listen. If ever a creature needed companionship this was it; but who would spend time in the company of a guinea fowl unless it was another guinea fowl? I made up my mind that it must have a mate, but until it declared its interests one way or the other, I was powerless to provide even that basic comfort.

Cocks have more red on their heads, I had no doubt. But, I asked myself as it disappeared from sight behind the fold yard, than what?

Country Matters

Living without a man constantly to hand makes, in the long run, for a better relationship with males in general. I am able to accord them the respect due to them in those fields where their superiority is apparent, seek their assistance and advice when I feel the need and offer what aspects of female companionship are proper to each situation as it arises without the need for prior consultation with anyone at all. For me, most of the time, it works.

I freely acknowledge their occasional necessity, however, and in the case of domestic livestock, kept under a degree of unnatural restraint, the provision of an acceptable male, and thereby the means of annual increase, falls to the one who has assumed responsibility for them. Take the goats, bless them.

At the end of the first summer, when Emily's milk supply began to fail, I was recommended to ask the advice of a local lay preacher, one of whose sons was looked upon as something of a goat man. He agreed to lend me a billygoat for as long as might be necessary. I thought it strange that anyone would trust a novice with valuable livestock, not realising in those early days that the billygoat, or at least the billy of no particular pedigree, is one of the most expendable, and therefore most abused, of the creatures that change hands among the keepers of domestic livestock.

Later that day, a small van came to the house, and from the

20

back there gazed the gentle, long-suffering face of the first male goat with whom I had ever been in anything like intimate contact. Nigel.

He was Nigel the first time I laid eyes on his gentle, intelligent expression. He was dragged out of the van and misjudged the distance to the ground, falling and grazing his bony knees on the tarmac. 'Pay when you've finished with him,' said the driver, and whirled away leaving me holding the malodorous Nigel on a bit of frayed string.

He was a real gentleman, of perfect temperament. When the van came again to take him away I watched sadly as he was unceremoniously loaded and trundled away. I wondered what would become of him.

The year following the success of Nigel's visit, I enquired once again of the same man and was told that there was indeed a billygoat available and that he would be delivered as before. I hoped secretly that it would be good old Nigel again, and was disappointed to be told that it was not, although I could see the wisdom of sending another, as some of Nigel's daughters would be among the ladies waiting for him. Nigel had left us a lovely little nanny and, although I hoped that she would not be served that year, you couldn't be too careful. I had no doubts that I should be able to handle the billy when he arrived, as Nigel had taught me all the rudiments of management by his wise and gentle handling of my inexperience. He had prepared me for all the problems I might face except one. Stinker himself.

For Stinker he was, by name and nature, this sulky, slit-eyed beast whose only similarity to dear Nigel lay in the remarkable sameness of the bit of whiskery string round his damp, yellow throat. The young man led him into the building I indicated and tied him to a wood trough. 'Cheerio,' he said, and went whistling back to the van. We were alone together.

I looked long and hard at Stinker, comparing him with Nigel, who was all I had to compare him with. He had once been white, but the male goat's habit of spraying urine over his front legs and beard had turned both these the colour of a chain-smoker's forefinger. I noted the look of scornful dislike in the yellow barley-sugar eyes which seemed to have nothing to do with the rest of him. It was as if his real, satanic self was somehow concentrated behind the black, horizontal slits in the centres of them and was watching from within like an urchin peeping through a letter-box, waiting for his chance of revenge.

But there could be no revenge to fear from this beast, since I had never wronged him, and I decided to begin our relationship by offering him increasing amounts of personal freedom until he began to abuse it. I untied the string from the trough and held out my hand to him. He drew back, but only for the briefest moment before rising on his hind legs to throw the whole of his considerable weight behind his menacing horns, which caught me across the top of the thigh as they slashed sideways and down. It was agony. As he rose again for another blow, I dodged out of the building, and even as I pulled the door shut behind me, he cannoned into it and I heard the wood splinter as he ground his great horns deep into the boards.

Nigel had had horns, but they were an adornment, something to hold onto him by. I had never thought of them as potentially dangerous and never really looked at them in that light. I looked now. Over the top of the door I peeped, hardly daring to breathe, but Stinker was no longer taking any notice of me. He was busy smashing the trough to pieces with the horns which were, on his murderous head, weapons of fiendish effectiveness.

They rose straight upwards from his brow to a height of about three feet, their tips turning outwards and backwards so that he would be able to scratch his behind with them, which is what Nigel used to do. Not round, like a tup's horns, not smooth like a bull's, they were triangular in section, with the front surface forming a ridged cutting edge.

This point of design, coupled with the undeniable expertise of their exponent, made them spine-chilling.

Cilla had had horns. Cilla was a fat maiden aunt of a nannygoat given to me by slight acquaintances before I was experienced enough in the ways of goats to know better than to agree. She was a sort of fleabitten grey with a broad, stupid face above which the slim, spiky horns rose like exclamation marks underlining the overall foolishness of her expression. On Cilla, the horns were neither threat nor ornament, but only a terrible inconvenience. She once almost hanged poor Emily by thrusting one of her horns under Emily's collar and then panicking. On several occasions she was discovered trapped fast by those horns in a small lilac bush that grew in the yard. Day after day I would see her struggling like the ram in the thicket, but she usually managed to free herself without much more than a few minutes' struggle. One day, however, she appeared to be having more difficulty than usual, and I went to help her. It was then that I saw what exactly was holding her fast. It was a short length of baler band, tied in a reef knot.

Years later I discovered that she had been in the habit of racing my neighbour's cattle for their ration of cake and winning more times than was good for her. I never asked whether this had anything to do with her frequent sessions in the lilac bush, but merely assumed that this was his way of evening up the odds. Horns, to a nanny goat anyway, can be a handicap.

Stinker's horns, however, were a threat to life and limb. More particularly to my life and my limbs, since nobody else would go near him. Visitors peeped over his door like sightseers at Newgate viewing the confined felons, and it became apparent that it was females and children to whom he was especially averse. A man would see only a sullen, brutish smelly animal, skulking in a corner of the building, but a woman would be attacked without hesitation. And above all, it appeared, he hated me.

Anything I had touched was anathema to him. The plastic buckets in which I brought his water, being afraid to let him out, were systematically smashed to pieces one by one. Each day I would lead the nannies up to his door and observe carefully, scanning them for any signs of interest. If any such sign was shown, I would open the door just wide enough to admit her head, and while Stinker was investigating, I would shove my knee firmly under her behind, push her inside and shut the door, all in one trembling movement.

The preliminaries to mating in the goat are not especially tender. The billy approaches the nanny with his top lip curled back in apparent disdain, then thrusts his face at hers while uttering a strange staccato grunting. He strikes at her with his forefeet, not so much to be aggressive as to give her the full benefit of his personal stench, and then, if she will accept him, he mounts and serves her. In a gentle old billy, or an awkward young buckling, the procedure is not without charm, but Stinker made even those brief encounters rough and unmannerly.

If the nanny, once she had been served, does not hold in kid, she will return to the billy anything from sixteen to twenty-one days later, so someone who is running a borrowed billy would normally wait till that period has elapsed since the last nanny was served before sending him back, just to make sure. Thus, grudgingly, I resigned myself to hanging on to Stinker.

There was a white frost on the morning of the day after his last conquest. I let myself out of the door and went into the yard to start on the daily routines of checking and feeding. I heard him before I saw him. A revolting paraphrase of the rutting call; a clatter of devil-hooves on the tarmac. In seconds he was in the yard, swinging in for the showdown he clearly longed for. I threw his water-bucket at him and ran. Stinker was out.

Even with that realisation came another. The post was due. Our village postmistress would at any moment be speeding down the hill all unsuspecting on her shiny bicycle towards the very spot where Stinker waited, pawing the ground and sending short sharp clouds of dragon-breath into the frosty air. Luckily this was before they disconnected the telephone and I was able to forewarn Mrs B. with a message to a neighbour's house, but all the same I was able to see the fatal meeting in my mind's eye as clearly as if it had really happened.

Even to this day I cannot quite decide where I found the courage to tackle that gruesome goat. I remembered reading that when dealing with a billy one should keep in mind at all times that he has neither the size nor the power to kill or maim, but I found this of scant comfort. Nowhere did it say that he could not cause fairly grievous bodily harm while trying, nor did it, in so many words, discount the possibility of his terrifying one to death. The only way to catch Stinker was to stand my ground as he charged, seize the fearsome horns as they struck and then hold on tight. The first time my courage failed and I side-stepped as neatly as a matador while he thundered past, reared and whirled for another try. This time I got him. I can remember pushing him backwards like a runaway wheelbarrow every step of the way to the building from which he had escaped and barricading the door behind him with all the heavy objects I could find.

For the second time that day I went to the telephone and dialled with shaking fingers. I spoke to the preacher. 'Send someone to get that billygoat,' I said, trying not to betray my panic. 'Please.' 'Has he done his job?' he asked. 'Yes,' I said, a little too readily. Then I remembered the status of the man I was addressing, so I added, 'I think so'. He went on talking and I listened with numb horror as he assured me that there was nobody else waiting for Stinker, and that it would be quite in order for me to keep him until I was sure. Only the truth would sway him. 'I would really rather you came for him,' I began, trying to keep the edge of hysteria out of my voice at the thought of another three weeks of Stinker. The preacher seemed to be having some kind of coughing fit and it was some minutes before he could speak clearly enough to say 'Why? Has he been a bit naughty?' and that was all he did manage to say before he was robbed of speech once more. It was agreed at last that Stinker would be collected as soon as possible.

It was a beautiful night, cold and clear and made even better by the arrival, shortly after dark, of the young man who owned the billygoat. He stepped unarmed into the building and arrested Stinker while I went into the house to fetch the fee. 'It's a lovely night,' observed the young man, as he pocketed the money. 'Do you like to look at stars?'

I suppose it is all the practice I had being ill as a child, staring at cracks in ceilings, but I am one who, given a few moments looking at any group of stars, would be prepared to swear that I could see in it any shape you might care to mention. Like Hamlet's cloud. I love the night, just for the nightness of it, but I have never found a lot of romance in the stars. 'Mmmm,' I said, but I was watching Stinker.

He had made several direct murderous attacks on my person yet now he stood obsequiously behind his owner on a hairsbreadth of baler band, eyeing me up and down. Was he wondering about a parting thrust with those terrible knife-edge horns?

The young man stepped a little closer and put his arm round my shoulders. 'Can you see the Great Bear?' he asked. His cheek was almost touching mine and the night was breathless and still. One time when perhaps I could have enjoyed the beauty of the heavens. But the yellow eyes were on me like the finger of fate. I disengaged myself from the arm of my charming companion and said grimly, 'Never mind the Great Bear – you keep your eye on Capricorn!'

All the goat societies and most of the available books on the subject seem at pains to point out that it is the duty of the goat-keeper to use, as far as possible, the approved billies standing at stud in the area. None of them seem to see that this limits the available talent by rather false criteria and leads to inevitable inbreeding. It does seem strange, since in so many cases what is good for sheep is good for goats, for the goat people to converge annually on a single billy while the hill shepherds go to considerable trouble and even more considerable distances to bring in tups from far afield. All the same, I did try it once. It provided me with a nightmare journey in the back of a Landrover which I resolved there and then never to repeat.

A kind young neighbour, hearing of my need for transport for this worthy purpose, offered to run me over to the nearest stud billy when the time was right. I sent him an urgent message — 'tonight's the night', as it were — only to find that when he arrived his wife had decided that it would be unsuitable for him to travel at night with me and did not seem to think that my own three children provided adequate chaperonage. The front, and only, seats in the vehicle were occupied by the good lady and her own children, and since I could not leave mine unattended we all piled into the back where we parked ourselves gingerly on the icy metal floor. A goat in season is not a comfortable travelling companion and the goat in question was a cantankerous creature at the best of times. This was the worst of times. She wailed and fidgeted all the way to Pickering, voiding copiously at unnecessarily frequent intervals. She made the most of her brief encounter and stank all the way home.

The following year I bought a white billy kid whose only positive qualification was the fact that he was totally unrelated to any of my own goats, and when his job was done I fattened him and had him slaughtered. I found the results satisfactory and the meat delicious. And so we proceeded, each year introducing new young talent until I was tempted to keep an especially attractive one for a second year, having sold all his female kids. He died of enterotoxaemia the following spring.

I was sorry to lose him, but did not foresee any difficulty in replacing him when the time came. Wrong. It proved almost impossible. The goat trade, till then something of an anachronism in being one of the few aspects of livestock trading not entirely sullied by big business, had gone completely mad. Suddenly everyone who had goats seemed to be grappling their way up a tottering ladder of herd improvement leaving fewer and fewer entire billies available to the honest amateur, the registered ones being priced out of the reach of those to whom goats are simply a cheap and cheerful milk supply and the 'scrub' billies all being destroyed or castrated in the furtherance of the cause. I drew blank after blank and retired, defeated, to think the matter over.

The problem was that I had two female goats whose oestrous cycles were not synchronised, and no billy in view. I might be able to persuade someone to transport one of them once, but no way could I con anybody into doing it twice, and enquiry proved that if I parked the pair of them on some billy's owner for three weeks, the charge would be astronomical. I decided that the sensible thing to do in the circumstances was to get hold of the nicest billy I could find, at whatever the cost, and offer his services to likeminded persons at such rates as would defray a little of the outlay without resorting to the charges mentioned by the goat-Hiltons I had contacted.

I asked a local livestock dealer to help, and within a few days he rang to say that he had found a billygoat. The following day I went with neighbours to pick him up in Northallerton and I was as excited as if it were my own Mr Right I was going to see. From the window, before I left, I could dimly make out the figures of the goats sleeping in the yard and I smiled to myself as I thought how delighted they were going to be.

He was beautiful. I had agreed to buy him sight unseen and was prepared for a degree of disappointment, so I could hardly believe my luck when I was confronted with a light-boned, long-legged animal whose overall appearance had that indefinable air of quality. Everything about him, from his slender, silky neck to his long, flicked-up ears, was pleasing to the eye and I was delighted with him.

'What sort of billy is he?' I was asked by one of the friends who hoped to make use of his services. 'White, hornless and willing,' I replied. He was also, in the final analysis, totally unable. If I and my fellow cottagers trusted our springtime increase to him, we were all going to be disappointed.

This was a sad surprise to me, and to the man who had sold him to me, not to mention the poor nannies, but to one person it came as no surprise at all. My friend Peter, who at that time was eight years old, told me from the very start that he had doubts about my new billy. His reasoning was simple. Buoyed up on my romantic notions of the handsome stranger stepping into the lives of the patient nannies and sweeping them off their skinny feet, I had named him Galahad and that, as Pete pointed out, was where I had made my big mistake. Pete was something of an expert of Arthurian legend and was at pains to convince me that Galahad was the only pure knight of the round table, remaining, to the end of his life, uninspiringly innocent. Thus, he assured me, unless I was hoping to grovel out the odd grail from among the bramble bushes, and assuming that I was entertaining him in the hope of issue, Galahad was, as names go, ill-advised.

I didn't really believe him, of course, but all the same I tried to change the name we had chosen. We all made a gallant effort to refer to him as Lancelot instead, but Galahad tripped so readily off the tongue that it was soon apparent that this would be his name, take it or leave it, as long as he remained with us. After all, it was nonsense – 'that which we call a rose by any other name would smell as sweet' – and another nagging little thought came into my mind. For a billy in the rutting season, Galahad smelt very sweet indeed.

At Swainby sheep sale I met young Mr T. who had sold him to me, and asked conversationally 'Is he a guaranteed worker?' 'Aye,' he answered, 'when he isn't asleep!'

The problem now was how to wake him up. I asked our patient vet for a course of hormone therapy and, although he pointed out that this was unlikely to solve the problem since the spirit was already willing despite the flesh being weak, I tried it. Close scrutiny detected a slight increase in belligerence, though this might have been straightforward objection to being pierced in the fundament as a regular sort of thing, and a vague strengthening of bouquet which might have denoted an increase in glandular activity. The first of the visting nannies arrived and offered herself utterly. Galahad all but took her up on it. But all but isn't enough.

I telephoned young Mr T. and told him what was happening — or rather what was not happening. I was at pains to point out that in no way did I consider it his fault — after all, Galahad was a lovely example of a Saanen-type buckling and there couldn't have been any better-looking than he was in the collection from which he had been picked. To his eternal credit, he said at once that he would put matters right somehow, and that I would hear from him before the next Wednesday. Wednesday being market day at Northallerton, this is the day on which most matters of this nature are settled. On Tuesday evening he rang to ask me to take Galahad back to Northallerton. He, for his part, would bring two more billies and I was to have my choice of these and give back Galahad in straight exchange. A shining example of honest trading. The people who took the telephone message offered to take Galahad in their trailer.

Mr T.'s pick-up was already in the car park and two voices called in doubtful harmony from under the canvas top. As the area was full we were forced to park at the farthest point from it as the crow flies and the haltered billygoat hobbles.

When I was a small girl in navy knickers, we were subjected, as part of the eleven-plus selection, to something they called the Intelligence Test. I did quite well, I recall, but was none the less beaten hollow by my great rival Tony Barton. After the test we compared notes and he explained airily the solution to a problem about a farmer, a goose and a fox, all of which had to be transported across a river and there was only one order in which it could be safely accomplished. I wished I had listened to him then. I wished even more that I had him with me in the car park.

We had one billygoat, A, in a trailer, X, and two billy-goats, B and C, in a pick-up, Y. Somehow, A had to change places with either B or C and all was to be accomplished fairly swiftly as Mr T. had almost finished his business at the mart and wanted to go home. I thought along these lines as I pulled on a set of waterproof clothing I had brought with me – after all, I still had some shopping to do and I couldn't very well walk through the Co-op smelling of billygoats.

The most important thing, I decided, was to ensure that I left Northallerton with the billy most likely to succeed where Galahad had failed. Therefore I left the latter where he was and went to get a better look at the alternatives. There they sat in the pick-up, two fat, white babies who sucked greedily at proffered fingers, and my heart sank. They seemed so young. All the same, the air around them was thick with promise. If they proved as potent as their pong my troubles would soon be over. Goats mature very quickly – a billy kid can get stock at three months old and if he is not serving at six months he probably never will, and I set about choosing.

The tests I applied were many, personal and best left uncatalogued. I couldn't stand upright in the pick-up and crouched in agony, trying to manhandle one of them into a manageable position while the other chewed unhelpfully at any unprotected part that presented itself to him. I had a felt-tip pen in my pocket to mark my chosen one so that I could return to the trailer for Galahad without having to choose all over again when I got back.

I could feel the corners of my mouth twitching at the ridiculousness of the whole thing and when I made my decision and told the little chap of my intentions – 'You're the one that I want' — I said to him — I was suddenly reminded of a popular song of that title and began to sing it aloud as I dabbed blue dots all over his wrinkled nose. Two people returning to their parked car quickened their step visibly.

I squeezed out of the pick-up and returned to the trailer for Galahad. He was wearing the only collar and I had to attach the halter to it and get him back to the other two before I could transfer it to my chosen substitute. Now came the moment of truth. I couldn't drop the back door of the pick-up because there was a trailer attached, impeding its descent. I would have to open it as far as it would go, lift Galahad bodily, depend upon a beady glare to hold the other two immobile while I shut the door and changed the collar over, open the door again and somehow hold Galahad and the rejected suitor while I made my escape with the chosen one. It just wasn't on.

In the end, two complete strangers offered assistance and stationed themselves either side of the half-open door while I effected the transfer.

Back at home, the new billy took over the leadership of the little herd as though he had always been there. He was just as pleasant as Galahad with his human contacts, but to his nannies he was as bigoted a male chauvinist as I have come across, and they loved it.

He was shorter and squatter than Galahad, but otherwise quite similar and the children suggested we should call him by the same name. I disagreed.

It was not as if I attached any credence to the ridiculous theory of young Pete. It was just that I felt Tarquin suited him better.

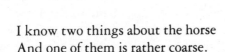

Horse Nonsense

I know two things about the horse
And one of them is rather coarse.

Although my eccentricity developed at a fairly early age, I was still a normal enough little girl to experience that almost universal longing for a horse of my own.

Horses have always fascinated me. At the age when I began to wonder about Santa Claus and faced the fact that I would never make a name for myself in County cricket, I still cherished the belief that I would one day join the Royal Horse Artillery and drive a gun-carriage. When the hard fact of male chauvinism put an end to that dream, I turned my imagination to world-class show-jumping. Even now I sometimes see myself side by side with an honest Clydesdale homeward wending my weary way.

But I no longer see myself in the saddle. A heavy horse in harness still makes my heart miss a beat, but the sight of a saddled pony now brings a feeling of tension to the muscles of my thighs and an ache to my buttocks. I was cured forever of my equestrian daydreams by a master of aversion therapy. I had him on loan while his owners were away on holiday. They called him Spangles.

He looked like a circus pony, gaily piebald, with a square, dependable appearance. Every inch a safe and solid mount, until you looked into his eyes. They were odd. Literally odd. One of them was limpid brown, wise and vulnerable, the eye of man's faithful servant. The other was a cold, calculating Arctic blue.

To do him full justice, he was a truly dependable mount for little ones. Trudging at a pace somewhat slower than my own, he bore his little hardhatted burdens with an air of defeat like a seaside donkey. The only way his pace could be increased in these circumstances was by carrying a bag of sandwiches just in front of his nose, but this smacked so strongly of the donkey-and-carrot technique that I never had the nerve to adopt it on the main road for fear of being caught.

He suffered children with torpid indifference, but not a fool gladly, and he knew me for one the first time I tried to ride him.

I was told that one should always put on the bridle before the saddle, but not before he had already shown me that there are few sights more ridiculous than that of a woman running after a saddled horse with a bridle in her hand. I had been told that the reins were the means of guiding the horse where one wanted it to go, but I found my technique so unsatisfactory that it was more expedient to get off and push.

As to increasing his pace when actually aboard, I was at a total loss. Drooping along like a pit pony on overtime, he steadfastly ignored tentative rein-flapping and encouraging geeings-up. His blue eye swivelled heavenwards in a mute appeal to divine justice against the idiot in the saddle. I got the feeling that he was perfectly well aware of what I wanted, but was suspending decision, like a mother with her hand poised above the sweet jar, waiting for the 'right word'.

I found it by accident. In the course of the urging and joggling, I clicked my tongue against the roof of my mouth and he broke into a spine-shattering trot which he kept up for about fifty yards before subsiding again to his amble. I reminded myself that he was on his holidays.

He had a profound dislike of going down hills. Since our house lies in a valley, this presented something of a problem, which I solved by tacking in the manner of a racing yacht in great zigzags from the road gate to the front door, which process took some twenty minutes. I felt, however, that I had begun to get the measure of him.

But he, too, had used his time well, and I found that he had worked out a definite plan of campaign designed to dissuade me from practising my horsemanship on him. It was all based on the element of surprise. He was a past master in the art of the split-second thistle-nibble that made his entire front end disappear, leaving me poised, terrified, on the edge of a horsehair cliff.

Once, when we were negotiating the bridle path below the house, at the sort of speed one would normally associate with an octogenarian pushing a three-wheeled pram, we halted, by his inclination, at a point where a grimy rivulet, the overflow from a field drain, crossed the path in a grudging trickle. 'Three faults,' I asserted bravely and dismounted, stepped over and pulled. He leaned back in an attitude of Thelwellian determination.

I backed him up, to avoid the necessity for a three-point turn, and tried again. He stopped once more, leaning down to peer myopically at the offending obstacle, which was no more than the width of his hoof. I patted his behind encouragingly and he rocked backwards, then hoisted his forequarters from the ground and took the thing with an exaggerated leap which would have cleared Bechers Brook with a yard to spare. I dare swear that his chagrin at finding me still in the saddle was matched only by my own amazement at the same fact.

In a burst of confidence occasioned by this apparent evidence of supremacy, I trundled him out into a nearby hayfield where the bales were stacked in seventeens ready for leading home. I had the intention of using them as obstacles round which I would steer him like a pony club bending race. I was going to let him know which of us had the upper hand. Unfortunately he already knew.

I aimed him between the first pair of stacks and he began, unbidden, to trot. I wheedled him towards the second pair and he swung into an effortless canter which took him straight past them. And then I heard the thunder of galloping hooves, like a cowboy film on a television set in another room. I realised, with a sense of horrified detachment, that it came from beneath me.

The trees at the bottom of the field hurtled to meet us. I wondered academically what would happen when they arrived. I lost a stirrup and hung on to the front of the saddle. My posterior rose and fell in a rhythm not synchronised to his, so that as I landed back in the saddle, it rose to meet me and made contact with a force that bounced me up again like a dried pea dropped onto a drum.

I was no longer landing dead centre. I was tipping inexorably sideways and there was nothing I could do about it. I realised that we should have parted company long before the trees arrived. I was sprawled on his neck only inches from the wild, blue eye which was now glowing with an inner fire of fiendish pleasure. One more bounce and I flew in a gentle forward arc to hit the ground with unimagined force. I did not remount.

They say time heals all, but I have never seen myself in the saddle since that day. At the time I even resolved never to meddle again in the mysteries of horsemastership, but twelve months later that determination crumbled, not in the face of some vision of equine perfection, nor at the sight of some mighty agricultural powerhouse, but before the steady brown gaze of a Shetland colt. I bought him, and named him Magnus.

I met him first at a farm near Thirsk, where he lived with his mother and a multitude of aunts and cousins. In a field nearby a collection of young hunters displayed, even to my uninitiated eye, all the angular grace of a Stubbs original.

Beside them, the Shelties could not be looked upon as noble
or beautiful with their rough, rotund, economy-pack bodies
mounted on solid utility legs, but in their cheerful company
and obvious good humour there was comfort for the likes of
me. What better tonic for the painfully unhorsy than the
proximity of this, the unhorse?

I had spent a lot of time that spring cutting peat up on the
moor above the house. I hacked it out, sliced it up, carried,
spread, turned and ruckled it, and then saw it all spoilt when
the weather broke before anyone had the time to lead it back
for me. I needed a vehicle for jobs like that. Something to do
the job, not of a tractor, but of a wheelbarrow. The idea grew
in my mind until it led me to that paddock where the aged
mare nipped the round little bottom of the colt who stood
taller than herself, maintaining her authority firmly but with
the minimum of bombast. I filed that picture away as my first
lesson in colt-handling and agreed provisionally to buy him.
I had a month to make up my mind.

I wanted him, but not with the desperation of a little girl
waiting for Santa Claus. I tried to see him, in a year or two,
carrying peat and firewood. Hauling hay up the moor to the
sheep, striding beside me through snow and rain.

I had no way of knowing whether this hairy, sprightly
youngster would ever fit that image, but I knew that the pony
I wanted would have to be cast on-site from available ma-
terials and the black colt with the exuberance of youth in his
step and the wisdom of centuries in his dark, mellow eyes was
the likeliest piece of raw material I had ever seen. So I
decided to give him a try.

The people from Thirsk delivered him. He stepped from
the trailer dripping with sweat and smelling of fear. When
the car drove away with the empty trailer clanging up the hill
behind it, I realised that the skills he would have to acquire
were a mere drop in the ocean when viewed beside the
amount I had to learn. As we faced each other over the
glowing billows of golden straw in which he sank knee-deep

I realised all over again that I knew nothing at all worth mentioning about the horse.

I amassed an armful of beginners' handbooks on the subject and read till my head ached. Doubtless the writers were explaining everything in full, but they all seemed to find it necessary to do so in the exclusive language peculiar to the subject and totally unfamiliar to the true novice, and time was to prove that the worst pitfalls are those never pointed out by the initiated, as they must seem too obvious to mention to those who have already fallen victim to them and profited by the experience. Like the business of the wind.

Magnus and the wind had more than a nodding acquaintance. Possibly due to the emotional stress of sudden weaning, he passed it at varying intervals and in extravagant quantities, with a noise like a market trader ripping a bolt of leathercloth, and a lingering aura that haunted the pasture for some time after he had wandered away. It was not a constant habit, more an occasional response to an inner need, but when one night I located him after dark by nose alone, I looked up the problem in one of my caring-for-ponies publications. There it stated, quite categorically, that raw potato, chopped up, was good for the wind. So I plied him daily with little piles of shattered tatty to no noticeable effect.

Mentioning this to a neighbouring farmer who has a wealth of experience in these matters, I was told that the word 'wind' when applied to the horse refers to the breathing of the animal. I was humiliated, especially since, fearing that I may have been too euphemistic in my description of the problem, I had looked it up under 'f' and even, just to make sure, under 'ph' in the impressive index. But although I was introduced to girth-galls, spavins – bog and plain – and bridoons, the only word that seemed to bear any relation to the subject under consideration was 'wind'.

That problem was never solved; it was merely supplanted by another. He had still not been with us for very long when another neighbour, quite unaware of his presence, drove a flock of sheep down to the dipping tub beside the house. With men shouting and flapping jackets and dogs running at full stretch to outflank them, the sheep poured down the hill like woolly porridge boiling over the lip of an invisible saucepan.

This was a sight I loved and I stationed myself to watch them, but poor Magnus, inured though he was to cattle, children, cats and low-flying aeroplanes, had never seen a sheep in his life. Before I realised what was happening he had raced as far as he could across the yard, away from the white wave that was rushing down to engulf him and launched himself at the wire netting that served for a boundary fence.

He lifted his forequarters up and over, but had not the strength to clear it entirely. One of his hind legs became entangled between the top of the netting and the single strand of high-tensile wire which topped it. I raced to help him as he hung there and it was only a matter of seconds before I had him the right way up again. It was a very subdued pony that I led back into the yard, but I assumed he was simply reacting to a chastening experience and I gave him some hay and went to help with the dipping.

Such a tiny incident in retrospect, and it was a day or two before I realised that there were to be any repercussions. Then I noticed him standing oddly. One leg was held bent, and he touched the toe of his tiny hoof to the ground as though he were dipping it in treacle. When made to move, he dangled the leg as though it were shorter than the others and he was clearly in pain. This merited a visit from our dear long-suffering vet, whom God preserve, of Northallerton.

I told him what had happened. He looked grave. If it had been an older animal, he said, it would have meant a trip to the knacker, but youth was on his side. Rest was the only cure, and only time would tell if even this could effect a complete recovery. I was to ensure that he did not trot or gallop; that he ambled sedately through the next few weeks and suffered no further frights. As he drove away up the hill and I was left once more along with Magnus, I felt cold and wretched. This was the first animal I had ever owned that had come perfect and whole to the smallholding and I, through ignorance, had crippled it. I practised telling the neighbours with a grin how he was never going to make a shepherd's pony if he was afraid of sheep, but it had a hollow ring to it. I didn't feel very much like a shepherd then, anyway — more like a damned fool.

By the end of that week his pain was obviously great and I called the vet again. He left me some powders labelled 'for the pony'.

Once, long before, I had presented one of his junior partners with a somewhat dilapidated duck which was clearly in need of medication. This was prescribed, but the young man murmured gloomily that he wasn't sure how I would 'get it down the ruddy duck'. I told him to leave that to me and felt quite in command of the situation as I tucked it under my arm like a set of bagpipes and trickled the stuff into its beak, which was no harder to prise open than the little plastic chute on a salt canister. But as I looked at the shiny packets of pony powder in my hand, I knew with a sinking feeling that this wasn't going to be easy.

It was not as if Magnus was especially obstructive about such things — on the contrary, he manifested a genuine desire to please. But how to go about convincing him that he would please me by consuming what looked like a half tablespoonful of sifted flour gave me pause. I poured some into the palm of my hand; he sniffed warily. Then he sneezed hugely and I went to fetch the rest of the packet.

Mix it, said the instructions, in food. I thought over the range of possibilities. Sprinkling it on the grass was never really on and the other things he ate in the course of the day are all dry and it is his habit, I have observed, to snort impressively at what he is offered which would effectively disperse any medication which I might have added beforehand. I thought of blowing the powder down his throat, but I had the sneaking suspicion that he might blow first and then I would have to decide whether to send for the knacker or enter myself for the Derby.

Something moist was indicated, to which the stuff would adhere while being masticated; I recalled from horse fiction days something called a bran mash. So much attention was paid to its administration in the stories I read as a child that I believed for a long time that this was what made Black Beauty talk. I looked it up in my books.

I could probably have made one with the panache of a master chef, a cordon bleu creation to tempt the palate of the choosiest equine gourmet after all my researches, but when I enquired further as to its indications I was told that its usual use was for the Saturday night supper of working horses and that it was designed to keep the bowels regular. Since I was to adminster these powders twice a day it was clear that the bran mash was out. After all, regular is reasonable, but a twice-daily dose would make him downright monotonous. And I had already proved the limitations of the raw potato.

The answer I came up with will probably never find its way into the veterinary manuals, but it was a complete success. I spread a slice of brown bread thinly with sticky jam, then dredged the dose onto it. I clapped a second sticky slice on top and then cut the whole thing into 'little soldiers' of the sort I used to dibble in boiled eggs as a toddler. These, fed as goodies, disappeared down without touching the sides.

The drug had a magical effect. Under its influence Magnus relaxed the tensed muscles, moved freely around the yard without that horrible hobbling gait and ate all that was put before him with renewed appetite. I no longer had to watch him suffer, but this proved a mixed blessing. Without the pain as a constant reminder of his limitations he would, if unrestrained, do forbidden things. He felt well enough to jump and scamper, acting the fool as he had always loved to do, but to do so, the vet warned me, was still as dangerous as ever. I myself now had to take the place of the restricting pain.

How he must have hated me. He grazed only on a lead-rein with me on the other end of it, and when I was unable to be with him, he was confined to his loosebox and yard. He fretted.

At this time there roamed the fields about the house a big, cheeky tup lamb whom I had christened Korky. He had come down when the local sheep were gathered in for tupping, but he was a stranger from the other side of the moor. The Swaledale tups who were busy ensuring the next crop of lambs were fine fellows, worth, collectively, quite a bit of money, and so young Korky, still entire and ready to prove it at the slightest opportunity, was a great embarrassment. He was an ugly-looking animal, but since his owner was not to hand, nobody felt like taking the responsibility of castrating him. I had offered to hold him under house arrest until the day of the forthcoming sheep sale at Swainby, when his owner could be notified. The only place I had to confine him was Magnus's loosebox.

Magnus was delighted with him. All his fear of sheep was forgotten as he shared bed and board with Korky. At night he lay relaxed and happy with his head resting on the lamb's woolly back.

Sheep were a good trade at Swainby that day. Some of the tups made over a hundred pounds and most people came away satisfied. I, too, was pleased with myself, because Korky's owner had sold him to me.

When the sale was over, a somewhat sarcastic daleslady asked me loudly whether I had bought anything. 'Just a Swale tup,' I said in an offhand way. I walked from the sale field in search of a lift home, and I knew that the buzz of conversation I left behind was concerned largely with that piece of news; after all I had only a tiny handful of Swaledale sheep, so what could I possibly want with a tup of my own? I bet they thought I was daft.

Mind you, if they had realised that I had bought him as a present for a pony, they would have known for certain.

The Oneness of One

When it finally became apparent that my husband and I could no longer live honestly together as man and wife, the decision to part was more of a relief than anything else. Looking back, I can see a great collection of faults, reasons and excuses of which I was, at the time, only half aware, and the visits to the solicitor, the drawing up of agreements and the actual, physical, bit-at-a-time parting, easing the children gently towards acceptance of the idea that their father now lived somewhere else.

It had its lighter moments. In an agony of mistrust, I scanned every word of the agreement drawn up by my husband's solicitor, the layman's natural mistrust of legal jargon increased a hundredfold by the heightened irritability of a mother under threat. I had to have the children.

When I first read the terms of the document I was horrified to see that the provisions for maintenance of the children were to continue only so long as I 'remained chaste', which struck me as a bit of a liberty. The solicitor had anticipated my reaction and appended an explanatory note. The clause was simply meant to ensure, he said, that I would not continue to take money from my husband while being financially supported by someone else. If anything that was even more distasteful. It was not my chastity that was being called in to question, but my amateur status. I said so. The solicitor replied condescendingly, explaining that this clause had its roots in legal history and was known as a 'dum sola dum casta' clause, and since it was too complicated to explain, he would delete it, but he needn't have bothered. My legal knowledge is nil, but I do know a little Latin — enough to translate that phrase as 'While she is alone, she shall be chaste'. While alone, I thought cheerfully, it would be difficult to be anything else.

I have never been much of a mathematician. If anyone were to cut off my hands I probably would never count anything again. Not that I have to stick up my fingers and count them down again like your more honest simpleton; I have a more subtle method whereby I tap out the domino pattern of each number on the palm of one hand with the fingertips of the other. I find it quite impossible to visualise a number without this surreptitious tactic, and it is only in recent years, when pocket calculators have become standard schoolroom equipment and it is no longer considered cheating not to do sums 'in the head' that I have dared confess my ineptitude openly. I am also, as you will appreciate, completely unable to cope with numbers greater than ten.

I remember being greatly comforted in my disability by the assertion of an erudite friend that the whole problem stemmed from the way I had been taught mathematics at the outset. Too many children of our generation, she said, were taught multiplication tables as a magic formula without ever being made to understand the very soul of mathematics, the spirit of the numbers themselves, the oneness of one. A small unquiet voice within told me that perhaps the multiplication tables, had I ever mastered them, would have proved more efficient than my imaginary dominoes, but I stilled it with that magnificent piece of educationalist cant. After all, what chance had I ever stood without appreciating the oneness of one?

Again, it is only in recent years that I have begun to realise that oneness has a meaning distinct, as it were, from

44

twoness, though not perhaps in the academic abstract my friend had in mind. The oneness of one at the head of a family where once there were two is a huge and unwieldy solitude.

I discovered at once that the role of the single parent is not a dual one — combining the basic aspects of both mother and father — but something quite separate, shaped by the bureaucratic sub-culture that has grown up round it. It is that of a depressingly sexless third party and, although I have learned to play it with a degree of panache, it still sits a little uneasily on shoulders ill-designed to support its complexities.

Because I live alone with three children and an Old-MacDonaldry of dependant creatures, people suppose me to be a tower of strength. Bureaucrats, sizing up my family circumstances, delight in setting up obstacles and, through channels of communication unknown to the layman, they arrange for all their booby-traps to blow up simultaneously in a triumphant culmination of their strategic skulduggery — a sort of personal D-day such as I occasionally live through and as a result of which I feel my sanity seriously at risk.

On one such day, my daughter was reading aloud from the *Oxford Book of Nursery Rhymes*. Her fancy was taken by an old lullaby telling how Mummy had gone 'to grind thee some wheat to make thee some meat' and my younger son remarked that you can't make meat out of wheat. The elder pointed out that you can, though, make a fairish approximation out of soya beans. They joined forces to adapt the rhyme, three heads bent over the book, red, blond and brown, and suddenly I felt lumpy-throated and rather tired.

On the table beside me was a pile of letters. Each represented a wild and desperate return stroke at one of the balls volleyed by the system. Tennis balls, my Liege . . .

There was one to the Electricity Board, who wanted to change my ten-pence slot meter for a fifty-pence one and I was resisting bravely. I had mapped out a working love-hate relationship with that meter just as it was and a five-fold increase in its appetite didn't bear thinking about.

There was another to the Department of Social Security. Their techniques have a subtle fiendishness that terrifies me, and I ceased dealing with them just as soon as I was able to embark on a period of paid employment, but they were not ready to let me go. They wrote to tell me that the Secretary of State had deducted money they owed me from money I owed them and that I had been weighed in the resulting balance and found wanting to the tune of a frightening sum. I failed to see how, if I owed them money they could owe me money at the same time, or vice versa. The people who call their arrangements a scroungers' charter should think again: they are a well-organised test of the mental fibre of the nation's honest poor. The letter I wrote detailed the minutiae of my income and explained that, if they really wanted repayment, I should have to apply for help from the Department of Social Security. Or, possibly, the Mafia, which seems to be the only other organisation able to threaten with impunity.

Letters explaining, cajoling, begging and hedging. The last one was to the District Council. They had written to thank me for paying my rates and enclosed a form to reclaim the sewerage rate I had been paying under protest since I came here. I had to hand it to them — it was a real beauty.

Not only did I have to tell them where all the water went when it left the house, I had to indicate it on a little pre-drawn map, which had a sketch of a house and a road. These were obviously the same for all applicants and I had had to write a note explaining that there was no way I could make their sketch fit my house, or vice versa, and suggested it might only confuse matters if I drew on it at all.

Then I had to tell them where the septic tank outlet went — so far so good. But the surface water? I assumed this referred to what came off the roof into the gutter, down the fat drainpipe and into the drain-hole below. But where after that? A grovel with a curtain-rod proved that it didn't join up with the house drains, but nothing else of value.

The only thing to do was to connect a hosepipe to the standpipe, put the free end down the drainpipe and await developments. After an hour or so a small fountain appeared just where the old garden wall once stood. Now I knew both where the water went and why the wall collapsed. I filled in the form accordingly, but didn't suppose the District Surveyor would believe it for one moment.

And then the children wanted help with their current problem. Wearily, I suggested 'Mummy's busy bashing beans, for that's what textured protein means . . .' and, poor dears, they laughed and said I was clever.

This physical oneness has more obvious drawbacks as well — there are some jobs that cannot be done by one person alone. Someone once told me that they found inspiration in my ability to cope with adversity; several others have made it known that they find my failures far more interesting. The story that follows is, I'm afraid, one for the majority.

Mind you, if only I'd had the chuckling majority to hand on the night I decided to move the piano, I wouldn't have begrudged them the odd ho-ho if only they had been prepared to put their collective shoulder to the wheel when I gave the order.

As it was, I ended up with the piano stuck across the bottom of the stairs, supping gratefully at a cup of tea which Nancy, after squeezing under the keyboard to reach the kitchen, had made and passed over the top of the monster before daring to return within striking range of the mother who was clearly on the verge of violence.

The hardest thing to face was the fact that the wheels which needed shouldering were only a couple of inches across. They had steadfastly refused to turn all the way across the carpet and then, when I had grappled the brute onto the quarry tiles at the door, they suddenly remembered what they were for and trundled merrily in all directions like those fingertip ball castors.

In order to shift the piano into the back kitchen, it was

clearly necessary to shove it halfway out of the sitting-room door and then lift the inner end while turning the whole thing gently in the direction of the kitchen door. It came in that way, dammit. I took a deep breath, lifted, and then those wicked little wheels gave a squeal of glee – wheee-clunk – and the whole issue sped forward like a well-oiled wheelbarrow and hit the opposite wall with the force of a battering ram.

I was bested by a mere instrument. Mind you, it was the better part of an hour before I admitted that.

I clearly couldn't leave it overnight between the children and the comfort station, so I inched it back into the sitting room and slid it against the nearest wall, facing the place where it had stood hitherto. There was nowhere else it could move without putting itself in check either from the sofa or the bookcase, and the diagonals were covered by the doors. Stalemate.

The piano actually belongs to Nancy. When her friend Caroline looked like taking her piano studies seriously, her parents bought her a new one to play on and gave the old one to Nan to play with.

I have only myself to blame. I was the one who accepted it on her behalf, smiling welcome to the four strong men who coaxed it, like a great wooden cuckoo, into my poor little nest.

Strange how a piano that was fairly tuneful in a carpeted, centrally heated house sounded, in ours, as though it were being played in a public lavatory. Not even a pleasant bar-room jangle. None of your occasional duff notes. No, its lower register grunted in ugly discord while its high notes clacked dully, like loose false teeth.

You didn't even have to play it. I only had to raise my voice in ladylike protest at some minor breach of discipline and the strings started a mutter that rose to a discordant boom, upstaging me utterly.

Until that night, it stood outside my bedroom door and on

many a morning I had pranged my undercart on the corner of its keyboard and even, rising early, put the flat of my hand across one of its upper octaves when the lid had been left open. I would feel it grinning in the dark. So I thought that if I put it in the back kitchen Nancy could play it there while I sat in the sitting room enjoying its absence.

But it beat me, blast its wheels, and now it looked like staying exactly where it was until the next time I had four strong men to hand, which happens about as often as Halley's Comet.

So I tried it from the other angle. I have observed, over the years, that the difference between success and failure is very often simply a matter of how you look at it. I closed one eye and looked carefully. The first thing I saw was the long, useful flat top, high enough and firm enough to make a safe place to put our little Christmas tree, with plenty of space for parcels alongside. And the dark wood really did show off Granny's ornamental brassware a treat. In its new position it could no longer impede entry to my bedroom, and with the lid down, so you can't see where Nancy numbered the keys with felt-tip pen in the course of devising her own musical notation, it really did look almost presentable.

And if I had installed it in the back kitchen, I would no longer have been able to escape to the cooker when things got the better of me. No, all in all, I decided, I had had a lucky escape from what would have been a most undesirable course of action. By the following morning I couldn't for the life of me recall why I had wanted to move the dear old thing.

That next evening, however, visitors came. Three adults and two children and these, with me and mine, made a crowd, to which were added later Caroline herself and her Aunty Mo. The little sitting room was bursting at the seams when Caroline threw up the lid and began to play chopsticks with the fierce determination which, in other circumstances, is one of her most endearing characteristics. I began all at once to remember. But I fought it.

Over a year later, I was sitting looking at it, talking in the quiet tones that were necessary in its presence since anything above a determined whisper made it echo like the ghost of a West Indian steel band. I suddenly noticed that the pillars supporting the keyboard could be quite easily removed and that if this were done the sideways elevation of the dreadful instrument would become L-shaped, rather than oblong and it would then be theoretically feasible to shove the keyboard out first, wangle it partially up the stairs, then manoeuvre the bottom part into the passage and tip the great beast end-over-end until it was in the same position in relation to the back kitchen door, whence it would be a straight run to the great outdoors.

I awaited the arrival of the next visitor with ill-disguised excitement. I would solicit their assistance with the piano. It would soon be all over.

And there you see, was the flaw in the plan. No visitors. Not of the kind suitable for shifting pianos. As I tried to explain to our vet when attempting to arrange a bit of basic maintenance for our dear old pig, it's not that there's any shortage of strong men about, but women who are prepared to lend them, no questions asked, are few. I would do it alone.

The main difficulty about this part of the plan was the fact that the piano, while it stood on four dear little castors when upright, was not provided with any such refinements on the side, so that once it was tipped over, it became a dead weight and ten times harder to move. I tried to avoid tipping it until the last moment and succeeded only in getting it poised on two of its corners and wedged precariously in the doorway, ready to drop like a drawbridge on any unsuspecting entrant. No good at all.

So I borrowed a sack-barrow — a sort of railway porter's trolley, with cast-iron wheels and a protesting squeal built in. On this I trundled the upended piano, like a beached whale, into the required position.

When I got it into the back kitchen, though, I wavered. I had had an accident with a water pipe some weeks before, leaving a horrifying hole in the wall too high for any of the existing furniture to hide it; but if I balanced the china cabinet on top of the piano. . . . It was reprieved.

Mind you, I regretted it as soon as I had got it set up, but by that time it was too late. The ghastly thing had long since been past playing. The awful damp in our house had made all the notes doleful and flat and lifted the edges of the plastic ivory on the keys. When I am depressed, it only takes a little sympathy, a kind word, to buoy me up again, but once those keys were depressed, there they stayed until you took a screwdriver to them.

In the early hours of one damp summer morning, I heard a strange noise. Someone was playing that piano, notes sounding at tuneless random, eerie and forlorn. I went out into the kitchen, but the lid was shut, the keys still. I had to move the wretched piano, china cabinet and all, and remove the fusty cloth from the back of it to extract the terrified mole from its workings wherein it had sought refuge from Pootle the cat, who brings them back alive.

It would have to go. I had recently bought some new green paint, a lot of those posh tiles-on-a-roll and a bit of kitchen carpeting. I was going to do wonders to that kitchen, once the piano was out of the way. I got it as far as the front step but was unable to hold it and off it went; base over apex into the yard with a sorrowful boing. There it would stay until someone, somewhere, helped get it out of the way entirely.

Then we went to a farm sale and I bought a stonebreaking hammer. When we got back, Andrew was very depressed because he hadn't been able to go potato-picking and he needed the money desperately for a bass guitar, without which his group could never make the charts. He was sitting in the yard, twanging hopelessly on the back of the piano like an angel at a loose end. I handed him the hammer and his face shone. For ten glorious minutes there was no sound save the crashing of a frustrated teenager on a frustrating instrument, then we stepped out to see what we had left.

Hundreds of little wooden pegs, felt-tipped, which fit the Nine-men's-morris board a treat. A sack of lead weights that can be melted down in Marmite-lids and made into toy soldiers. A pile of wonderful kindling. A rabbit-hutch lid that lifts at a fingertip touch. And a huge square bit with strings on, which had to stay where it was for the time being, as it weighed a ton.

That night I heard the old, woeful sound again and looked out. There in the yard, ghostly-pale in the frosty moonlight, stood Googie the goat, poised like a gazelle on the piano-strings and paddling gently from one foot to the other, lost in thought.

The ability to fight seems to be a necessary attribute for a singleton if life within the community is going to be worth living. Sometimes I have had to shout very loudly indeed to drown the rough music.

Rough music, you must understand, was the way that country communities in earlier times showed their dis-approval of any individual whose conduct was displeasing to them. They would gather together in groups, beating on buckets and saucepans, leaving the unfortunate one in no doubt of their collective feelings. The targets of these out-bursts were usually the recluse, the eccentric or, as my reference book puts it, 'the woman playing what they felt to be a sexually inappropriate role'. Apparently, somewhere along the line, I qualified.

Not that I got the saucepans or the rowdy gatherings; rural society has progressed beyond such overt demonstrations.

It was more of an irreguluar tide of unstated opposition, particularly from the ladies of the dale, when my oneness and the manifestations of it proved especially irksome to them. At such times I became 'she' or 'Madam' or even, when things were especially bad, 'Her at Hagg House'. I had the freedom to wander about and the undisciplined lifestyle that allowed that freedom to be constantly indulged. Thus I always knew when and where things were going on and, because I spent so much time contemplating my surroundings, I was usually more aware of them than other people, so it was more often than not 'Her at Hagg House' that brought tidings of the cattle in the cornfield, the heifer in trouble with her calving, the whereabouts of an afflicted sheep or, on occasions, the sheep herself. My oneness has brought me, now and then, mockery, resentment and even a little fear. Once, after such a reaction, it occurred to me that I am the stuff of which, in former times, witches were made.

Perhaps this was what the villagers, delving deep into their folk-memories, stumbled upon to suggest to them the idea of asking me to act as fortune-teller at their annual Summer Games.

I don't receive many letters. Robert once suggested that this might be because I don't know many people who can write, but I am more inclined to the belief that the greater part of my circle of acquaintances lies among the nation's honest poor and is daunted by the postal charges. Thus, when I found a small brown envelope lying in the old hen-hut at the top of the hill, I seized it eagerly. It turned out to be a breakdown of the expenditure and profits from that year's Games, a glittering statement of overall success, but the envelope was addressed to Gipsy Rose Drysdale and I experienced a definite twinge of retrospective nausea as I recalled the occasion.

I am not sure who conceived the notion of having a gipsy fortune teller for the village's annual celebration, but on the face of it it didn't seem too bad an idea. Somewhere among the blossoming days of May and June, happily discussing plans on the telephone, I felt no reason for not giving heart-felt support to any of the proposed ventures. I was even happy to agree that, if nobody else would take it on, I would act as clairvoyant for an afternoon. After all, July was a long way off, and I was only going to step in if nobody else would take it on — but nobody did.

July loomed. The very day grew nearer. I began to sleep fitfully and threw myself into haytime chores with an unprecedented fanaticism in a futile effort to blot the rash promise from my mind.

Messages arrived intermittently. A caravan had been borrowed; a costume devised. Would I like the loan of a pair of earrings? Was I ready? Was I heck as like, but a promise is a promise, and I clung like one drowning to the doubtful conviction that it would be all right on the day.

I was collected by the wife of one of the organisers and her young daughter who, as a particular friend of mine, had secured the questionable privilege of borrowing my most mischievous little goat as an addendum to her fancy dress costume as Heidi. The brass bell round its neck clanged like a knell all the way down to the village. Ask not, I thought miserably, for whom the bell tolls.

Half an hour to go and I changed into the gear — an extraordinarily revealing top bought at a jumble sale in aid of the Heavy Horse Preservation Society, a skirt made from a length of borrowed curtaining and two curtain rings suspended from my ears with string. Somehow I crept along West End and into the caravan. Once ensconced, I laid out my crystal ball — a glass net float found at Whitby and prised from its tarred string bag for the occasion. The caravan was parked at a steep angle and the crystal ball rolled crazily off the plywood table and disappeared. I was on my knees, haunches heavenward, when the first customer entered and coughed. I stayed where I was until the coast was clear.

For the next half hour the caravan was full of children, asking me what I was going to do when a real customer came. I wished I knew. When a head appeared round the door my stomach shrank to the size of a walnut, but it was only one of the organisers depositing a borrowed beercrate in front of the step so that the elderly and infirm might enter more easily.

But I dare swear that nobody there that day was more infirm than I. I wished for Armageddon or a total eclipse. I had grave doubts as to the success of the venture.

When the first client came in, my fears were justified. I gazed into the crystal ball, fascinated by my sweating palms and much magnified grimy fingertips. Apart from this my mind was a total blank. Worse, when I did find something to say, it was greeted with a chorus of smothered giggles from the assembled youngsters outside. I closed all the windows firmly.

I decided to stare at the knees of my clients and if they were brown I would declare sepulchrally that they had just returned from a journey and, if white, that they were about to go. After that I played it by ear, trying to sum up the people in turn and give them a pleasant thought to take away in return for their donation to Village Hall funds. The uncanny thing was that, after the wildest gropings of imagination, a light would come on in the hearer's eyes and I would be told with authority what it was that I had meant by it. I told a total stranger that she would have good news of the health of a loved one, and she told me delightedly that I was referring to her asthmatic grandchild. I told another that a big change for the better would come in spring and she confided that she had just had confirmation of the presence of a longed-for baby. The children were the hardest of all. How does one please a child with anything less than a specific promise?

In a fog of terrified misery I ploughed through the afternoon until emotional drain made the need for a cup of tea so pressing that I shut up shop and retired to a friend's house, slipping all the change from my purse into the takings box as a sop to my conscience. Walking ahead of me in determined pursuit of something were two special constables. I watched in horror as they converged on my little goat who had slipped from a shed and was blissfully demonstrating its imaginative topiary along a row of rose bushes in front of a parish councillor's perfect garden. While I removed the cause of the disturbance, someone else removed the beercrate and the deposit had to be deducted from the meagre takings. So much for clairvoyance.

But the deepest wound of all was inflicted later. When I was asked by an elderly neighbour whether I had met the new wife of our respected gamekeeper, I replied that I had not yet had that pleasure. 'Oh, yes you have!' The old lady's eyes twinkled. She was obviously enjoying this. 'You told her fortune at the Summer Games!' I turned cold. What had I told her? 'Oh,' she said, grinning, 'simply that she could expect a bit of good news at Christmas!' So when that letter came I thrust it deep into my pocket and went for a walk. Gipsy Rose Drysdale — in a pig's eye!

Having convinced my local critics that I am quite without occult powers, I have then to contend with the unsubtle hints of some who believe that by living on my own I prove myself a deviant from their standards of sexual behaviour, as if by building my own walls, spraying my own brackens and gelding my own lambs I make of myself a sort of hermaphrodite or freemartin. My trying such things they cannot understand; my occasionally succeeding they find it hard to forgive. I am quite a dab hand now with foot-rot shears, castrating pliers and de-horning irons, but not so good at driving home fence stakes or putting up shelves. I have no sense of the vertical or horizontal, so that all my fences have a truly rustic appearance and a tin of beans laid on its side on one of my shelves will trundle merrily along its length, drawing attention to its angle which can be anything up to forty-five degrees out of true. I am the world's messiest painter and my plumbing is a disaster. This last is a great pity, because I have been called on to do quite a lot of it, especially in the course of my running battle with our lavatory.

I don't seem to have a lot of luck with lavatories. I recall how, as a child, my whole day was governed for good or ill, according to whether I could get downstairs before the flush had finished, and many a scraped ankle and bruised behind that occasional dash would cost me. All across the country I left a trail of destruction during the family's infant days, as I proved time and time again that disposable nappies are only truly disposable when burned, buried or jettisoned on the high seas.

When I lived on the houseboat I well recall testing the newly installed sea-toilet, only to find that the non-return valve had been fitted back-to-front so that depressing the lever, instead of emptying the pan, caused a great tidal wave to surge from below, flooding the mid-section of the vessel to a depth of some eight or nine inches.

The cracked pan that was here when we arrived did not stay cracked for long. A year or two and a little piece came out of the rim. Another year and a bigger bit detached itself. These dilapidations, as they occurred, were combated with putty, cement and glue, but as jigsaw puzzles were never my forte I gradually ended up with a lattice-work pattern down one side of the pan and a fistful of spare bits on the windowsill.

This deterioration, like the growing-up of the children, happened so slowly that it passed unnoticed until a particularly weighty visitor strained the poor patched contraption past endurance and ended up on the floor amidst a sort of minefield of potentially lethal bits.

It was at this point that I discovered that of all the cliquey and secretive trades, that of the retailer who supplies plumbing necessities to the general public heads the list as the most devious of the lot. His lists call for a seasoned code-breaker and any request made simply and without ulterior motive of any kind results in a great burst of plumbarious terminology designed to belittle the potential customer until he truly believes that he doesn't know what it is he wants.

I knew perfectly well what I wanted. I wanted a lavatory pan. I telephoned a plumber's merchant and told him so. He said he couldn't supply one unless he could see what it was I was talking about and the cost of sending someone out to tell me what it was I wanted was more than the amount I had saved up to buy one.

I tried a relatively small firm and a woman answered the phone. I explained the problem and started to describe the variable part of my pan. 'It's no good,' she told me, 'unless I know whether you want an S trap or a P trap.' 'And your jakes is no good,' I told her acidly, 'unless it traps both.'

I finally found a gentle little man in the Yellow Pages who could understand what I meant by an outlet pipe which goes neither out at the back nor out at the side but straight down through the floor, and he came and put it all right for a tenner.

But it was another three days before the thing actually worked as I had attempted to save money by demolishing what was left of the old one, and had swung away with a sixteen-pound hammer as though there were no tomorrow. The works were thus blocked solid with shattered porcelain which had to be removed with borrowed drain rods. This took ages because the tools on the end of the rods were designed to cope with the more normal hazards encountered in plumbing systems. There's a wheel for stiff blockages, a rubber plunger for sludgy impactions and a corkscrew for whiskery bits, but there isn't anything specifically designed to remove coarse aggregate. For a blissful six months thereafter we had a proper flushing system as good as any anywhere. Then Our Robert, now a wiry mite, gave an unusually hefty tug and the thing-that-pulls-the-plunger came away in his hand.

On the telephone to the plumbers' merchants again, but this time at an even greater disadvantage. Try explaining that what you want is the thing that goes gershloom when you pull the chain.

Standing on the lid and reaching into the cistern, I could feel the hook onto which this thing fitted. A little upward tweak and it flushed as well as ever. There was just no way of operating it from ground level.

A neighbour told me that his father-in-law had given him a complete set of bathroom fittings to break up for hardcore, old but serviceable, and he was sure that the gershloom had been in situ the last time he laid eyes on it. This proved, however, to have been some three months previously and we fought our way for an hour through nettles bigger than both of us with no result other than what might be expected in such circumstances.

And then my brother came to stay. I am eleven years his senior, and for the first part of his life, I was the mender, the bodger, the putter-together and maker-better-than-before of all his broken toys. Once he wept over a broken plastic skeleton and I got a medical book from the library and made it an artificial hip-joint. Once I did an intricate growl-transplant on his teddy. Once I made pretend flames for his broken Spitfire so he could make believe the Messerschmidt had done it.

Now six feet five, bearded, a slaughterman, a poet and a father himself, I wondered how he would react to staying in this rough and ready environment. I wondered how my sister-in-law would feel about having a lavatory that didn't, if you see what I mean.

But when they left, it did. Time after time I pulled the chain and only the usual noise of flush and refill greeted my ears. I looked up and smiled at the mechanism itself; as sweet a piece of junior engineering as ever a little brother contrived, and all made of Meccano. Nevertheless, I pulled again and again, just to see it work, to see it spring upright again with just the suspicion of a shudder, like a railway signal. And over and over again I listened to that satisfying sound – gershloom.

Equally, you wouldn't think it was all that difficult to make a saw-horse. To hear the man in Sam Turner's tell it you'd think the average baby could mass-produce them in plastic Meccano in a matter of minutes, and that even the most feeble-minded of adults could manage one or two in a lunch-hour, given a few straight bits of timber.

'Two pieces like this . . .' he showed me with pencils on the counter, 'and a couple of cross-members.' It sounded too good to be true. All the same, I did a lightning tour of neighbours' woodpiles to run my apprenticed eye over their horses before attempting to create my own. I could see what the man meant. Two upstanding St Andrew crosses made of flat wood – fence rails would do – and a couple of parallel bars to join them together and stop them falling over. That really appeared to be all there was to it. The more I thought about it, the clearer I could see the saw-horse of my dreams, and I indeed needed it desperately.

I had found out that the sawing of long thin logs is a dangerous operation when there is no one to hang on to the free end, so off I went outside gathering up bits of flat timber to form the basis of my horse.

I poked about in the derelict buildings adjoining the house and soon amassed the necessary components – a bit off the cold frame I made two years ago in which I grew a few rather dismal marrows, two rails from the fence that blew down in last year's gales, a bar from a collapsed gate and another rather grubby bit of unknown origin that Nancy had transformed during the summer into a work of art with hours of painful squeaking and a borrowed brace and bit.

All these treasures I bore into the house and piled in the middle of the kitchen floor.

It took quite a while and much naggling with an ancient bow-saw to produce four pieces of reasonably equal length to make the crosses. I laid two of them in position and drove a nail in. It popped through both pieces and was brought to a sudden halt by the concrete floor. The last hammer blow before I realised this bent its poor head at right angles and I had to pull it out and start again.

This time I laid them on the milking stool and, although I hammered very gingerly, the nail went in such a treat that it fixed the wretched thing firmly to the seat and when I detached it it left a horrid little hole. Then, in order to get the angle of the second cross the same as the first, I laid it on top of the completed one and then found that I had nailed the whole blasted issue immovably together.

In the end though, I coped not too badly, and got the side pieces nailed on, after which, believing myself to be nearly home and almost dry, I made a cup of tea and sat down on my poor mutilated stool to survey my handiwork.

It wasn't right. Its feet weren't level.

You'll see what mean if you hold two rulers in the shape of a cross and stand one end on a table. It was quite clear that I needed to take a slice off each leg, at a bit of an angle, so that the horse would stand properly on four flat feet.

I got the bow-saw again, then had an inspiration. Why not use the chainsaw? It would surely save a great deal of arm-ache and I could see clearly what had to be done.

I upended the unfortunate creature smartly and zizzed four roughly equal lumps off the ends of its legs. Then I stood it up again. Disaster! In tipping it upside down I had sort of lost track of the shape I was aiming for and now it stood on four little wooden tip-toes, teetering at a fingertip touch. I tried again and ended up back where I had started. Twice more I tried. Offcuts piled up around me.

That night, for the first time, I used my little saw-horse. It wobbled a bit but it did the job admirably for all that. In fact it was perfect except for one tiny fault.

Its legs were a little short.

The Black Sheep
of the Family

There was a time before Snuff came. Nature being what it is, there will undoubtedly be a time after she has gone; but of all the waifs and strays that have passed through the dilapidated gate, she has made the greatest contribution to the success of the venture. Not only in a financial sense, although she has long since made nonsense of the local assertion that pet lambs always die in debt and has even provoked the surly comment 'T' bugger shits pound notes', but more especially by her constant presence as a reminder that, now and again, love really does conquer all.

She arrived in our kitchen in a cardboard box, an hour old, still wet, unbelievably small and black as funeral boots. The same black face still peers goodhumouredly at the world, but her wool is now iron grey, having grown lighter with successive shearings and with the action of the water that has flowed under the bridge since the evening when she lay, dried with a towel, primed with goat milk and castor oil – my only colostrum substitute – on the first rung of life's ladder. It looked unlikely that she would ever reach the second.

In the next few weeks, however, her will to live – or more precisely her determination not to die – pulled her through almost as many sheep ailments as my well-thumbed veterinary textbook could muster. On the evening of the fourth day of her life, I found her collapsed and shivering. Her breath came hard and rasping from her open mouth and she dribbled copiously. This was E. coli infection, the deadly enemy of every lamb that has not had colostrum from the ewe, but the diagnosis is a retrospective one. All I saw then was another little lamb dying from the painful, messy illness that had already taken several of my adopted orphans.

It was all going wrong, you see. On paper, it seemed good economics to use the spare goat milk to rear lambs to finance the moor flock I dreamed of, and in previous years I had been able to have the pick of any local foundlings. But all at once, the womenfolk of the dale rediscovered this among many other lost arts of farmwifery, and it was more than a man's life was worth to let 'her' have a lamb, no matter how sick and hopeless, so I bought lambs from newspaper advertisements, and in that disastrous year these expensive half-bred butchers' lambs failed one after another, and dribbled and shivered their way to death without much of a struggle.

Snuff was delivered as a makeweight alongside one of these. Her mother was an elderly moor ewe drafted down-country but not, as they say in the sale-ring 'correct below'. She had the disability about which small boys sing to the tune of 'Blaze Away' — she had but one teat and had borne twins. The smaller, weaker twin had been brought to me as a gift, 'for luck'. A black, towel-coated down cross lamb of the type known disrespectfully in these parts as Snuffolks. Hence Snuff.

On that night, though, there didn't seem to be a lot of luck about. I lifted her gently to say goodbye and laid her in her tea-chest by the fire. As I moved out of sight she raised her wobbly head and called feebly to the only mother she had known. So I tried.

It was 9 p.m. I fetched in buckets of firewood and stoked up an impressive blaze. I drew the chair up close and tucked her inside my shirt. For hours I held her, talking and singing: 'Little Lamb, Who Made Thee?', 'Baa Baa Black Sheep' — anything to keep me awake so as not to let the fire out.

Somewhere along the line I nodded off and awoke at 4 a.m., the fire glowing red and the little body in my arms quiet and still. Believing it was all over, I moved to lay her down and stretch my aching muscles. With a flurry of match-stick legs she struggled upright and demanded a belated supper.

At ten days she contracted a skin disease that blistered her lips until she couldn't drink. Her eyes were filmed over like the swollen glass in old shop windows, but still she blundered blindly after me, falling about like a Keystone Cop, suffering squirts and splurges of patent sprays and folklore unguents until her face was whole again and one eye quite clear, though she only regained a little sight in it and none at all in the other. She still steers awkwardly and constitutes a definite road hazard when approached on her blind side. Her extraordinary way of carrying her rather fine head draws comment from visitors, but we, the rest of her family, have ceased to notice it.

At six weeks old, she failed to join the morning milk queue. I found her up to her knees in the pond, drinking noisily. When I called to her she raised her head and curled back her top lip in sheepish agony. I lifted her out of the water and she collapsed, groaning. In the previous few days I had buried two other lambs after similar patterns of be-haviour had played themselves to what I now saw as an inevitable conclusion. I had thought it must be pulpy kidney disease or one of the other well-known pitfalls of which I had read, but this terrible, depraved thirst didn't seem to fit. I carried Snuff to a patch of shade and left her. When I looked out of the window she was standing under a blanket on the clothes line, sucking furiously at the corner of it as though the soapy drops were vintage wine.

In the textbook, after a tearful search, I found a straw and clutched at it. I measured a generous dose of worm drench into the miniature bottle I keep for young creatures and tipped it down her greedy throat. I laid her in a shady place, visited her and comforted her for an hour or so, then, as the spark seemed to flicker out, I said goodbye and left her in peace.

At teatime I found her in the kitchen under the table, wolfing down crispbread crumbs. She never looked back; I drenched my few remaining lambs and did not lose another.

The curse was lifted, but of the ten other lambs I had adopted, seven had died. Of those that had been mine from birth, only Snuff had survived.

But she belonged to me in a way that none of the others did, having had mothers of their own. She felt it her right to wander into the house and settle with the cats by the kitchen stove with quiet aplomb. She would tiptoe to the sitting room and peer blearily round the door until my voice betrayed my whereabouts and she would hurtle like a fuzzy torpedo to collide with my shins in an ecstasy of greeting, voiding prodigiously on the carpet, like as not.

Her medical history left its mark, though, both in her steadfast refusal to grow, which made nonsense of her voracious appetite, and in the little bald patch which appeared on her back and began to spread.

Not knowing that severe setbacks often cause breaking of the wool, I feared infestation and decided that she must be dipped at once. This presented something of a problem because the nearest dipping tub was filled with two hundred gallons of murky rainwater and the only dip I had was a drop in a plastic bottle on top of the kitchen press. I finally resorted to sitting the protesting dwarf in half a gallon of solution in the washing up bowl and squeezing it over her with a bath sponge.

Drained and drip-dried, with ruffs of wool round her neck and haunches, she looked like the early effort of an apprentice in a poodle parlour. I swung her out at arm's length and carried her to her companions. I set her down among them and stood for a moment, like the shepherd I wished I were, looking over my flock. Then, suddenly, Snuff began to dance. Like a black travesty of a carpet advertisement, she bounced in and out, tossing her blunt and ugly little head and kicking her pipe-cleaner legs in the sunshine.

For each lamb there is always a first time for skipping. For the hand-reared lamb it is the only true sign that they have decided to thrive, and it still thrills me to be present on such an occasion, even though none of them have given me quite as much pleasure as Snuff's ridiculous little ballet among the summer weeds.

Even so, while her three companions grew buxom and flirtatious, she remained small, and when I sent them to the next farm to run with a fine Suffolk tup I kept Snuff at home. I deemed her too small to breed and she would follow me across the fields each day to see the others and it seemed as though she would be a lamb forever.

It was well into December when she brought Walter home to meet me. Into the kitchen she scampered, followed by a large and extravagantly affectionate Swaledale tup who brought with him a generous measure of the special bouquet common to all his kind at that time of year. I happened to have present a rather distinguished visitor who would not have seen eye to eye with me over the entertaining of livestock in the kitchen and, while I felt pleased that Snuff had seen fit to bring her friend home, I did see his point of view. So I shut the kitchen door firmly and prayed that they would do whatever they decided to do with a minimum of noise. When I returned after seeing my visitor on his way they were lying side by side in front of the stove, chewing vacantly.

It was not long after five o'clock on a May morning, and there was a slight frost. I left a mark where I knelt beside the little black sheep whose lamb had been so eagerly awaited and who now stood very still within the circle she had trampled in her fruitless efforts, accepting the help which had been so long in coming. It was a classic malpresentation, the head and one foreleg of the lamb delivered, but when I laid hold of the lamb to see how best to help I felt the cold, dead weight in my hand and knew that I was already, far, far too late.

It didn't take much persuasion to bring forth a fine big lamb, but as poor Snuff licked delightedly at the warm hind quarters I could see only the swollen caricature of a face with its rigid grin, the perfect body that had everything but the vital spark of life itself and the picture shimmered in and out of focus through a haze of tired tears.

Back in the house I gave myself up to quiet despair. What sort of a shepherd would allow such a thing to happen? Worse, had I caused the disaster by over-generous feeding, causing the lamb to grow too big for her to bear? I had dreamed all along of twins inside that vast girth, felt the swollen udder with a satisfied certainty that she would rear her offspring adequately, and now all the loving and caring had collapsed into the dull misery of loss.

Outside I stood and looked up the hill behind the house to where Snuff had chosen to deliver her lamb. So near to the house — how could I have let it happen? — and once again the pain swelled to an unbearable crescendo as the preoccupied sheep muttered quietly to her dead lamb, then turned to graze in apparent confidence that it would wake and suckle soon. I had held the icy face in my cupped hands, trying to breath life into him for her and I knew there was no hope. It was nature's mercy that I would have time to come to terms with it before poor Snuff accepted her loss and gave herself up to her own grief.

I watched her settle down beside her beloved lamb and the surge of pity and remorse made me giddy. Dear blind Snuff deserved her fulfilment and I was powerless now to give it to her.

Up on the moor a lamb cried. The thin wail of newborn hunger tugged unmercifully at my bruised brain and I gave a wry smile at the thoughtlessness of chance. The cry came again and suddenly, wonderfully, there rang a little bell somewhere among my muddled thoughts. There was, after all, a chance for the miracle, but it would take work from me, co-operation and trust from Snuff and the goodwill of all the friends and neighbours, already working at lambing-time pitch, on whose mercy I was about to throw the pair of us.

The cries of the lamb ceased. He had found his mother. But he had shown me the possibility that somewhere out there might be another lamb not quite so lucky, one whose need for what Snuff had to offer was as great as her need to give it.

I went in, made a pot of tea, sat down by the telephone and on the stroke of seven I picked up the receiver, dialled Mrs A. and began to tell the story that I was to tell countless times to scores of people, every one of whom listened with sympathy to what must have seemed a tiny problem by comparison with their own troubles. I felt the healing power of fellow-feeling.

There were a few orphan lambs about, but they were older and already being bottle-fed. The odds against their fulfilling Snuff's need were high, but they were offered generously, along with much good advice and helpful suggestions. I dialled my way steadily round the dale.

Of course, I didn't tell the story as I have told it here. I told it baldly, coldly. I laughed as I pointed out what such an occurrence did to my overall lambing percentage and the desperation was, anyway, being steadily eroded by the goodnatured understanding. There was no need to describe the bitter taste of defeat, the pain of helplessness, to the people I was talking to now. They knew. If they didn't they would not stay in these hills year after year, quietly caring.

Many of them suggested that I try J.W., who ran his farm single-handed. He had a lot of sheep and little time to tend the weaklings. But he was outside and didn't answer the phone. I had by now worked my way down to the dairy farmers nearer the village. Some of them sometimes kept a few sheep. One of them was a particular friend of J.W. and tried his number on

68

my behalf. But he was still outside and didn't answer the phone.

I knew him slightly — once worked there a day or two in haytime — but he was a hard man to find. I tried his two sisters, one of whom told me that the best time to catch him was at lunch, and the other generously waived her prior claim to her brother's spare lambs and wished Snuff well.

When I finally spoke to him, he said cheerfuly that there were two pairs of twins, born that morning on the moor above his farm, and that he would split them up and let me have the smaller of each pair if that would help.

Would it help? My joy must have been apparent as I told him that I would be up to collect them within the hour.

That presented another problem. He and I are the only householders in the dale with no road transport of our own; I rang the local livestock haulier. He said I was a bloody nuisance and that he had far too much to do to be bothered with a couple of newborn lambs, but he would be over as soon as he had finished his lunch and would I be ready.

Together we followed J.W.'s huge green wellingtons across the crisp heather and he finally stopped and indicated a wary-looking ewe with a pair of tiny lambs. He pointed to the smaller one and smiled at me. 'That one,' he said. Somehow, clumsily, I caught him. He was a frail little fellow, all head and skinny legs. He felt like a woolly breeze in my arms after the massive lamb that Snuff still guarded in the hazel spinney behind the house. Into my mind slipped a shred of conversation overheard between two hill shepherds at lamb-marking time. 'Yon's a moderate little bugger.' 'Aye, but he's worth a lot of dead 'uns.' I held the little lamb very close and felt the thrill of life in him. I knew what they meant.

I caught the second lamb under a wall and went back to the others. This one had a patch of black on his thigh exactly like the one whose place he must help to fill. I decided that he would wear the skin of the dead lamb and take the first step towards the heart that must by now be beginning to break. Only then did it occur to me to wonder whether I would be able to persuade Snuff to accept them. Would it be that easy to make a triumph out of disaster, or was I making a tragic mistake with the two little lives?

My misgivings proved more than justified. It did not take long to skin the dead lamb, slip its jacket onto the chosen substitute and tie his legs loosely so that he would rise with difficulty like a genuinely newborn creature. It took even less time for Snuff, after a perfunctory nuzzling, to batter the little thing against the side of the indoor pen I had made her until I had to take him away to save his life.

Hours later, I was still trying. Sweat ran down my back, which felt as though someone had extracted a couple of vertebrae and welded it together again. Blood flowed freely from a cut on the bridge of my nose, where a flying forehoof had caught it in my struggle to sit the poor sheep on her haunches and introduce two strange lambs to the udder with which she clearly felt they had no business to meddle.

Somehow I reached round her bulk into the corner of the pen and dragged one of the lambs by the scruff of its neck up alongside, forced the teat between them, and hoped that instinct would prompt the terrified little fellow to extract a drop of nourishment before Snuff's struggles resulted in one of her pedalling hind legs connecting with his body to send him flying back into the corner.

While the poor lamb stood with the teat in his mouth like a thermometer, I reached out again to drag his companion forward and thrust the other teat between his waiting jaws, but as soon as I got him, the first lamb subsided miserably onto the straw, quite unable to associate this unnatural angle of approach with the search for food. I gave up and allowed Snuff to rise gently to her feet.

I tied a hurdle across the corner of the pen so that the lambs could retreat behind it. Each time I went to suckle them onto their unwilling foster-mother, I would find them huddled behind it, little Dalesbred faces peeping like monkeys from their cage. I decided to give it one more day.

The next morning, though, when I tipped Snuff up for another session, it was clear that something was far wrong. The big black udder which should, by now, have been shining and hard was soft and empty. Her milk must no longer be coming in as it should – emotional stress must have caused her to lose it. Worried stiff, I looked for the lambs. They were not in the safety corner, but cuddled against the side of the pen; not the hollow, empty lambs I had expected to feel – no, they were round-bellied and full, and in a moment of sheer happiness I realised where old Snuff's milk had gone. I righted her and held her steady, but it was true – she allowed them to suckle once more, just to prove it.

I spent that day in delighted disbelief. Thereafter I decided to trust her with them, and let her go free. I had not a single moment's worry that she would desert or reject them. I hurried to telephone their former owner to tell him the good news – but he was outside and didn't answer the phone.

Now and again, as the weeks went on, I would call Snuff home, for no particular reason other than the pleasure it gave me to see her blunder down the hill with her two snow-white followers bobbing behind her, springing on all four legs at once, covering the distance tenfold in sideways bounds and bounces.

Twelve months later, the moor flock I had dreamed of had become a reality, with the odd assortment of pet lambs and bought-in gimmers being introduced to the moor above the house, and schooled in what was to be their particular heft – the stretch of moor on which they and their descendants would, in theory, run forever. I had sent Snuff to a neighbour's Border Leicester tup, in the hope that she might rear me a pair of good butcher's lambs to pay for the winter fodder for the following year.

The red patch on her rump showed that he had served her, but the march of time proved that it hadn't done a lot of good. The very fact that her cargo was still within showed that the responsibility for it lay with the Swaledales who were working in the fields around the house when I brought her back.

It was Thursday and it was pouring with rain. Not the gentle, fluttery showers we associate with late April, but great draughts of relentless ice-cold water that blew in erratic, gusty bellyfuls that washed over the front of my house like the North Sea on the decks of a trawler.

Right in the middle of lambing time had arrived this worst of all possible weathers, and it was a depressing toss-up whether the sheep and lambs were better up on the moor, where the lambs would have the shelter of the heather and their mothers would go hungry, or down in the fields where the ewes could get what grass there was and the lambs would huddle in muddy corners, protecting each other as best they could from the never-ending rain.

But this, for one last year, was my neighbours' problem and my only part in it was to sympathise and keep my eyes open for trouble as I went about my tasks. I had only this one sheep to lamb and she, almost from birth, has had her own way of dealing with rain when it came. She stayed in-doors.

She had, by now, a magnificent fleece, which was com-pletely weatherproof. Inherited from her Suffolk father, it rose in a dense fuzz high above her flat back, and lay round her neck and shoulders like a great ruff, deep enough to swallow up a plunging hand. Although her skin, her tongue and the shorter hairs on her face and legs were still as black as ever, the massive fleece was now a grubby grey and she made nonsense of its obvious adequacy by steadfastly refusing to get it wet if it could be avoided.

Thus is was no surprise when my morning summons was answered by a cavernous bellow from the depths of the carthouse. I would not have expected her to be outside when it was raining.

Another of the peculiarities she developed with adulthood was this amazing voice. Not an ordinary, sheepish sort of bleat but a tremulous grumbling that rises to a discordant crescendo with a strange echo to it as though the old girl had her head stuck in a galvanised dustbin and was impersonating a rogue elephant to attract attention.

I was tired. The previous day I had taken Andrew to York for an interview at the school of both our dreams and it was only when he and the headmaster shook hands and agreed to meet again in September that I realised, swept up on a great wave of relief, how worried I had been. I knew at last that I had done the right thing in encouraging him to go it alone in the face of the relentless tide that seemed set to carry him into the huge comprehensive. My academic prejudices and my socialist upbringing finally acknowledged themselves at variance but in a state of truce, and I had even slept a little on the way home in the train. But I was still tired. Reassured by the familiar voice from the carthouse, I left Snuff's breakfast till last.

I fed the hens, milked the goats, got breakfast for the children and saw them off, then heaved the haynets onto my shoulder for the yearling sheep on the moor. There was no further sound from Snuff as I set off through the driving, chilling rain.

Nothing is wetter than heather on a day like that. Stiff, woody stalks snap up at every step and the dead leaves discharge their burden of icy drops with a shiver, just at wellytop level. However carefully you tread, nothing can save you. I led the sheep down to their pen at the bottom of the ploughed intake, slipping down the greasy headland with the rain soaking into my shoulders as my anorak decided that there are limits to showerproofery. I got back to the house wet and shivering.

It seemed only sensible to give Snuff her breakfast so that I could go inside, change and wrap my frozen fingers round a hot cup of tea. I called out. Again the reply came from the back of the carthouse, behind the woodpile. But not the usual ovine yoo-hoo, the companionable greeting of sheep to shepherd. It was the low, throaty mutter only heard by those privileged to live in the countryside; the special crooning of a ewe to her lamb. She came forward to meet me, looking smugly sideways at a single, tiny grubby lamb which picked its way grimly over the tumbled logs into the drizzly daylight. 'Beeeeeh', it said.

Suddenly I was overwhelmed with a sense of utter anticlimax.

I snapped on the light and looked into the corners of the carthouse. I fully expected to find another lamb. Surely this tiny, bedraggled thing was an afterthought – but all I found was a single cleansing, writing finis to the operation. I wrestled bravely with the lump of disappointment that stuck like an underestimated mintoe, swallowed in haste, somewhere in the back of my throat.

The only excuse I can make for my wicked ingratitude is that I was tired, wet and cold; in an instant I was bitterly ashamed of myself. I looked carefully at the newcomer. Forget the blocky butcher's lambs I had counted for five months before they were hatched. Look at the alternative the warehouse have sent us.

A gimmer. Black legs, black head. Crisp white curls with a sprinkling of black at head and tail. Gradually she came into focus like a view through someone else's spectacles. A white dot on the top of her round little head. Speckled ears. Just a few white hairs on her knees, like holes in black stockings. Nose and mouth like a child's drawing. Sloe eyes that shone bright and unafraid. Agnes.

A few drops of rain pearled the slubby fleece and Snuff muttered, nuzzling her back under cover and licking her dry all over again, scolding lovingly. I picked up this unsolicited sample and held it to my face.

As that long winter tottered into its tenth month, the feel of her blunt nose thrusting below my ear promised an eventual spring. She had the good feel, the clean, strong smell of a freshly laundered towel. So much life in such a tiny package. Our Agnes.

The Importance of Having Ernest

The goats were in full milk. It was the time of year to start taking on a new set of responsibilities. I had just had a particularly good sale with the previous year's pet lambs and I was anxious to try again, but silk purses are impossible to make if sows' ears are not to be had. I let it be known that the orphanage was once again open for business and that no waif was too small or too feeble to be considered.

The following night the telephone rang — had I a place for a hungry orphan, a place in my heart for a foundling in need of care? Of course I had, and said so, but as soon as I had put the telephone down I began to wonder what I had let myself in for, and I was once more stepping outside my experience. The newcomer was a pig.

He arrived in a very small cardboard box and when he was lifted out of it he began to squeal. He continued squealing while I attempted to feed him, gargling furiously with his good milk and glucose in a paroxysm of pink fury, for all the world like a human baby to whom no has been said with unusual firmness.

Having dribbled a little nourishment into the thing, I went outside to show the goats to the lady who had brought him, and the only way I could smother his shrieks was to stuff him unceremoniously up my jumper.

Later, alone with Ernest Pig, I told him that we should

have to come to some arrangement whereby he com-
municated his needs in a less nerve-rending manner and I
would then undertake to attend to them as promptly as
possible. He did not see eye to eye with me over this and
negotiations broke down in a crescendo of agonised squeals as
the pangs of his belly once more managed to convince him
that his throat was cut.

On reflection, it seemed unlikely that Ernest Pig would
ever see eye to eye with anyone over anything. His little eyes,
of a sad and watery blue, seemed set sideways in his head and
he groped myopically forward, prodding obstacles with his
cold, clammy little snout before making up his mind to hop
over them or to waddle round. He thrust it up the leg of any
available trouser, searching for the vulnerable bare patch
above the top of the sock, and then struck home with it as
though going in for the kill. Pigs' snouts look sensually
appealing and Ernest's resembled a pink rubber button of the
type that adorned my liberty bodices in more sheltered days,
but when he poked it tentatively at a piece of exposed flesh, it
felt like being attacked by a dolls' house sink plunger.

He was a particularly testy little fellow and hated being
picked up, preferring to leap off steps rather than be helped
down and jumping in the air like a frog-hopper in the
summer grasses when touched on his fuzzy back. It was not
long before he became bored with his box and would leap for
freedom twenty minutes after each feed, dropping squarely
on his cranium every time but seemingly not being much put
out by it. I became used to entering my bedroom cautiously,
peeping about to discover the whereabouts of Ernest Pig
before I crushed him to death with a misplaced foot.

On the day of his first public appearance I used baby lotion
to remove the few muddy marks from his face and dusted his
fuzz before introducing him to my neighbours. As they were
passing I called to them to wait while I fetched something to
show them.

Of course, when I went to look for him, Ernest Pig was not

to be found. Not under the bed, or in it. Not in his usual place sitting like a hunchback on the fender staring into the fire with his tail hanging down behind like an end of dish-cloth cotton waiting to be darned in. No, there he lay, pale and still, stretched out on the glowing coals. For a moment I dared not breathe, dreading the choking stench of burned flesh, dared not touch him for fear the charred skin came away from his ruined body. Then he sneezed.

I remembered that this was the fire sent as a present from Aunty-Mary-in-Dundee, and although I normally detest those imitation coal-effects only marginally less than flights of flat-backed plaster ducks, I blessed inwardly the sweet realisation that the glowing embers were in fact as cold as yesterday's rice pudding and would be of scant comfort even to a brass monkey.

But the wretched pig had been rootling up the chimney and I scurried out to show my waiting neighbours not the blossom-pink mini-porker I had so carefully preened for display but an enraged and squealing thing of indescribable filth of which I was by now deeply ashamed. I was relieved when he disappeared back into the house and my visitors commented kindly that he would soon be as big as a pound of butter. 'If,' I thought, 'he should live so long.'

In the end, though, like all little dependent things, he won his place here; it was his as long as he needed it. He went about grumbling like a cross clockwork mouse, and he was undeniably a demanding nuisance, but I came to like being woken, even at 5 a.m., by his rubbery little snout, and as every mother knows, there is a rare satisfaction in feeding the youngster who always cleans his plate.

One day a visitor asked after Ernest Pig, and this enquiry occasioned a period of agonising self-appraisal which would have had a woman of less stern stuff whimpering at the back door of the booby hatch. I am, I have concluded, some kind of thing apart — some feral anachronism quite unsuited to take part in the twentieth century.

The idea of anyone asking about Ernest is not in itself anything remarkable. The little fellow had a sizeable collection of admirers. He was by now round and solid, with a capacity for enjoying the simple things of life which I found most endearing. The sight of a full piglet, collapsed in a pool of dappled sunshine, is a symbol of such contentment that it is almost a privilege to witness it, and I had become genuinely fond of the lad over the weeks.

No, this was not the sort of polite inquiry as to his health to which I had become accustomed — the question concerned not his welfare but his whereabouts.

I had told everyone how I had kept the tiny thing in a box in my room, and my inquisitor was anxious to know whether, a month later, he was still there.

My first thought was that he hoped to meet Ernest, so I replied that he was now in the pig sty, but the relief on the face confronting me was so evident that I realised I had committed some misdemeanour in allowing him to share my night-time accommodation.

My next thought was that his objection was on some moral ground, but I dismissed this as ridiculous. Even the lady in the old ballad, who loved a swine, built him a sty of his own — albeit a silver one. None the less, I was told that the house was no place to keep a pig, and I wondered miserably how many other people had condemned me for this social indiscretion, the public confession of which bears witness to the fact that I saw no harm in it at the time.

After all, he needed constant warmth and regular meals, provision of which was made easier by his constant proximity to the electric fire and to his foster mother until he was big enough to move into a tar-barrel outdoors and then to his own stone sty.

It grieved me to think that those who objected to poor Ernest would probably be less bothered if it had been a couple of merchant seamen or the Northallerton first XV I had entertained.

A week or so later my sister confirmed that she was bringing her fiancé to stay for a few days. I viewed their impending visit with gloom. Would she be able to stand the company of one so lacking in social grace? Perhaps even at that very moment she was worrying lest she should be asked to share her bed with a broody hen or that I might embarrass her in front of her fiancé by chewing straws and muttering yokelries to myself as I stuffed the goat's back legs down my wellies and milked away into a chamber pot. What's more, I might have done.

In the course of the preparations for her visit I asked the twins to tidy their bedrooms − or at least to sort the treasure from the tat so that I might dredge through them at leisure to expose at least some of the pattern on the carpet which was, as far as I remembered, a rather pretty one. 'Why?' said Nancy. 'Who's coming?' − and I reflected that the mouths of babes and sucklings must earn their earholes many a clip.

None the less, I began to look around with new eyes, with the eyes of a critical visitor rather than those of the cheerful slattern with which I am wont to overlook rather than look over the immediate environment.

I saw the pile of moleskins on the step, the goatskins curing in a bucket of formalin in the corner and the collection of half-finished walking sticks behind the door. I noticed, in my first real look at the outside for a long time, that the weeds had begun to grow apace at the bottom of the step, that dandelions, groundsel and shepherd's purse sprouted wildly in gay profusion and there reigned an air of gone-to-seedery which was underlined by the sharp flourish of the first growth of stinging nettles under the wall. Only in one place did the tarmac show through dark and clean and that was where Ernest had rooted up the weeds and eaten them in his endless experiments to discover what in the world is tasty and what merely edible. His tail swung like a starting-handle as he worked himself up to do battle with the deep-rooted docks and erased the tender chickweed effortlessly with his india-rubber nose.

I went to his sty and sat beside him and he wriggled with pleasure as I scratched his well-upholstered body. Each day was adding another rasher to his rotundity, each dish of milk, each cold chip a broader grin to his guzzling chops. I had never kept a pig before, but was learning all the time and I honestly believe that I would not have had the chance to do so but for that little bit of extra care at the start. Most of my unthrifty little creatures come my way because of a reputation of being able to rear them, and the only secret attached to it is the capacity for loving them enough.

All the same, I was forced to catalogue Ernest Pig's early days among my many other social indiscretions, all perpetrated innocently and in the collection of experience. In future I should say politely, as the gauche do when they belch in company — 'pardon my pig — it's a friend'.

That was the long, hot summer of 1976. Week after week of sweltering, unprecedented sunshine and everybody made hay while the sun shone and when there was no hay left to make they began to pray for an end to the drought which prevented the grass from growing again and scorched the shaven meadows brown and bare. I suppose it is only to be expected that such weather should prove the subject of a great deal of retrospective grumbling — after all, what could be more upsetting to the English than a burst of fine weather right in the middle of summer?

Ernest was by now about eight weeks old, and the sunshine was affecting his exposed pinkness, drying and flaking the skin so that he itched miserably. We lathered him with dog shampoo, scrubbed him with a grippy nailbrush while he chuckled with pleasure and then attempted to rinse him off by throwning warm water from a bucket. We were amazed at his agility in dodging the drenches, and the children's squeals of glee as bucket after bucket swilled uselessly down the yard turned the whole enterprise into a giggling circus that left us with aching sides, stretched faces and the weak-at-knee feeling of having over-amused oneself, and with a clean, sweet-smelling little pig, rinsed at last with the occasional lucky shot and random ricochet.

Suburban families often react to the scorching of the front lawn by washing their cars, Sod's Law being enough, in most cases, to trigger off an immediate monsoon. In a rural environment, washing the family pig, it would seem, has the same effect. Within twenty-four hours it was dribbling down in satisfying quantities after an initial grumble of good-natured thunder that sent Ernest Pig scurrying on twinkling trotters to the safety of his sty, thence to peep in piggy disbelief at this dimly remembered phenomenon. He tried a few tentative rushes into this new downpour, dodging and swerving like an escaping prisoner through a hail of bullets, but soon realised that the odds were stacked differently this time and retired defeated, treating the changed scene to a particularly beady stare from the safety of his straw nest.

People will tell you that pigs have unsuspected depths of character and rounded personalities, facets of which are seldom shown to the world at large. Believe them. Once upon a time, young Ernest Pig was being shown to a group of visitors. He was still at the stage when even strangers would say 'Aaaaah', and as he busied himself like a clockwork novelty in and out of the polished shoes, nobody had eyes for the little black sheep who pottered with her fine new lambs in and out of that carthouse.

At some stage of the proceedings, Ernest poked his proboscis, like a pink two-pin socket, deep into the wool of one of the lambs, and although I realised that he was only checking to see if this was Tot Atkinson, the lamb who shared his accommodation and whom he regarded as his boon companion, Snuff was not prepared to give him the benefit of the doubt. She galloped into the middle of the yard and caught the trundling Ernest amidships. Over and over he rolled like a quarter of Cumberland sausage, and the fearsome black nose, curved like a Georgian bow window, dribbled him helplessly offstage left while one of the ladies cried 'Save him, save him!' and I, in response, rushed to tackle her and gain possession.

It had long been a source of amusement to the children that Ernest was, as they put it, a burglar-proof pig. At that stage in his development he would hop and squeak when touched in the small of his back and we showed it off as a party piece, but we tried as far as possible to avoid activating his burglar alarm.

It seemed as though lifting all four trotters simultaneously from the ground would trigger some kind of electrical circuit and he would squeal with ear-rending monotony until four-square contact was re-established and then he would continue his snuffling progress unconcerned, leaving the air ringing with his protests and every little noise of nature suddenly amplified in the blessed silence. Thus Snuff scored a try by depositing Ernest in the stinging-nettles at the edge of the yard and I converted by seizing him and conveying him with all possible haste to his sty, but the moments between the two were loud with anguished yells and effectively put paid to well-bred conversation for some minutes thereafter.

But it was all soon over. The visitors motored away; the pig dozed. Snuff steered her treasured lambs to less populated pastures and the silence was broken only by the mumbling of the old broody hen and the Asdic pinging of the guinea-fowl. And we forgot about it.

Some time later, during haytime, I was out in the fields stacking bales when the twins came to join me. They bubbled over with a tale of how Ernest had followed them as far as our neighbour's house but had been startled by their Landrover and scarpered with that incredible burst of speed that only a fleeing pig can produce. Their elder brother was, they said, seeing him safely home. Poor lad, he arrived half an hour later, hot and tearful, saying that Ernest had refused to go home and, when he lost his temper with him, had led him a very active dance over several fields before he had finally lost him in some bramble bushes. I imagined the scene but kept a straight face. Pigs, I told him, cannot be driven with sticks or hauled along on pieces of string. They must be accompanied in a friendly way and with no suspicion of coercion. We finished stacking the bales and set off to look for him.

I cannot deny I was worried. Ernest had never been so far from home before and I feared he would be lost. But there he was, safe in the yard, patrolling up and down in front of the carthouse while Snuff and her lambs stood on a stone shelf at the far end, marooned. She did not get down until I had taken Ernest back to his sty and soothed him with a bucket of something unspeakable, but she seemed not much worried by the incident. And we forgot about it.

Ernest grew prodigiously. He still regarded me with a great affection and sought out my company, but there were, as time went on, other aspects of him which were not so endearing. For instance, one day he stopped suddenly in his tracks, sniffed and listened. Then a swift plunge, a scuffle, and he had caught a live mole which he ate immediately. The dreadful crunch seemed to freeze the air for a few seconds and I realised fully for the first time the power of those strange pink jaws. His face seemed to be somehow singularly ill-adapted to the simple act of eating that gave him so much pleasure. I was forced to the conclusion, though, that it is our notions of pig-feeding that are ill-adapted to the poor pig. Preparing a rabbit for the oven, I picked up the severed head for disposal, but Ernest beat me to it, snatching the delicacy from my hand and demolishing it with a couple of crushing chews.

These are the creatures we feed with slops and mashes, but deep down in their pig memories are the days of the wild boar, most feared of man's adversaries. I began to treat Ernest with respect and I set a high value on his friendship.

A few days later, when I called up the sheep for feeding,

Snuff was limping. Clearly a front hoof was causing her extreme pain. I watched for a few seconds, then slid my arm round her woolly girth and stepped sharply backwards, sitting her up like a black kangaroo. I took the hoof in my hand for a better look. There was the round, silver head of a nail or tack of some kind. I concentrated, trying to get a better grip on the projecting head, when out of the corner of my eye I saw Ernest.

He approached with incredible speed. His mouth was open and his eyes wild, the rumbling beginnings of an almighty squeal bubbling on his lips.

One of Snuff's black velvet legs was dangling above his head and he made a snapping lunge for it. In a split second I remembered the mole, the rabbit and the humiliation he had suffered all those months ago. I pushed Snuff away from me and delivered a hamfisted karate blow to the side of the slavering snout and it was all over almost as soon as it had begun. Snuff wandered away and Ernest churgled happily as he scratched himself against my wellingtons. I made a mental note that it is not only the elephant that never forgets.

Autumn, and acorn time. A brief, fierce storm strewed the ground beneath one of the biggest oaks with tasty pickings for such of us as might be so inclined and I knew how pleased Ernest Pig would be with a pocketful or two. I knew too, though, that it would double his pleasure if he were to come and forage for them himself, so I decided to make myself a picnic lunch and share it with him in the shelter of the mighty tree.

Ernest and I set off across the two fields that separated us from the old oak. At the top of the second of them, two black cows grazed quietly. As we crossed the tufty grass to the muddy hollow below the tree, one of them raised her head and gave a low, moaning cry that rose to an angry shriek as she left her meal and began to trot purposefully towards us. Her companion joined her.

Now these were not strange cattle, but old and trusted

friends with whom I have shared most of my experiences. In my turn, I have shared in their triumphs and tragedies. I wander among them with pleasure and I am usually greeted with cheerful unconcern or even, from one or two of them, with little outbursts of nudging, tongue-swiping affection. But it was two of those good friends who were bearing down on me at that moment, and their intentions were clearly far from friendly.

It was Ernest, of course, to whom they objected, although I never found out why. They made their dislike quite clear as they stopped inches from me, dribbling angrily over the toes of my boots and peering at him as he squinted at them from between my legs. We stood thus for several minutes until, in an apparent effort to establish contact, he wuffed cheerfully at the nearest of the large black noses.

Another bellow of rage went up from the trees at the edge of the field, more and more cows began to gather and suddenly they were all running, heads tossing inches above the ground and the high-pitched note of complaint echoing round the valley. I stood my ground. The calves capered round, eager not to miss anything, and the older ones added their voices to the general disturbance. Only the bull himself stood apart and I appealed to him as the only apparently sane creature present to withdraw his ladies, but if he grasped my meaning, he was enjoying the situation too much to interfere.

It was difficult to move in any direction, because we were surrounded, and I hesitated to bring matters to a head by making a break in case Ernest was hurt, but didn't want to stay where I was for fear he lost his temper and nipped one of the aggressors. Then from the top of the field, the most terrible cry of all sounded out over the assembly. Old Beltie, the big belted galloway, had arrived to lend her voice and presence to the argument.

The ancient matriarch with her sagging belly, her daughter on her right, her grand-daughter on her left and her illegitimate great-grand-daughter, love-child of the bull across the beck, trotting behind her, began the sort of low, relentless descent of the hill that strikes terror into the advanced-upon and roots one to the spot. Then she gathered speed, raised her head for one last great rallying-cry, and broke into a gangling gallop that would have been funny if there had been a fence between us.

A look passed between Ernest and myself. As one, we turned and fled for the barbed wire fence and hurled ourselves through the smout-hole to fall in a heap, our heels scalded by the hot breath of our pursuers.

In the end, we sat on the doorstep and shared my lunch, meditating on the changing nature of things.

As the year drew to a close I could no longer escape the realisation that our beloved pig's days with us were numbered. There are really only two openings available nowadays for young male pigs – pork or bacon. Equally certainly, we could never eat him ourselves. A friend with a slightly fuller pocket came to take over his expanding appetite. As we waited for him to come, I let Ernest out for a last half-hour of his company. We went for a walk and he responded to the gathering dusk as so many domestic animals seem to do, with an outburst of mad energy. Up the hill he raced, as though anxious to meet his new owner. Up went his ears like a startled hare; down the hill he came again at his full glorious gallop, frisking like a lamb in summertime, shaking his ugly bullet of a head between my wellingtons so that he almost had me down. Tired at last, he indulged himself in a scratching session that drew his whole pink length up and down across my proffered foot while he wuffed with sensuous delight. And then he was gone. All we had left was a summer's good memories and a cheque for thirty pieces of silver.

Pig in a Poke

We missed Ernest more than we had ever imagined, and I promised the children, even before the tears had dried, that we would have another pig. A gilt. A Pig for Always, to fill the hollow place he left behind him.

Eventually, she arrived. Greatly longed-for and already loved, she was delivered at dusk by the people who had promised her since she was little more than a gleam in the eye of a Gloucester Old Spot boar and she was everything we wanted. Not that we wanted a lot, really, just Our Pig and each of us had our own private vision of what that meant.

So it was a very uncomfortable couple of hours that ticked slowly away between tea-time and pig-time and over and over again I thought of the old warning against buying pigs-in-pokes.

I quoted it aloud and asked the children what they thought a poke might be, and they all visualised it as an ordinary pen with pigs in, at a livestock mart or a farm sale. When I asked for a reason they painted a picture so sharp that I could only marvel at the clarity of their childhood vision.

Could I not, they asked, see the pen and the poor pigs inside, surrounded by grim-faced farmers, each one in his best boots and carrying his market-day stick. By the time they had finished explaining I could almost hear the grumping conversation. 'Yon's t'best of 'em.' 'Nay, be bug-

gered, yon's forever better,' and each remark punctuated
with a wave of the stick, each subject indicated with a jab
through the rails – poke, poke, poke. 'And if you bought
one of those pigs, it would be all little bruises where they'd
poked it,' finished Nancy. She threaded her arm through
mine and we watched for the car coming down the hill. 'Our
pig's coming straight from the farm, so she won't have been
poked,' she remarked happily.

But I still wondered. I told them that what people usually
meant by a poke was a bag, and that you shouldn't buy your
pig until you'd had a good look at it. I said that perhaps it
would have been best to go and choose her ourselves, that way
we would be sure she was just what we wanted. 'Like
Barbara?' asked Andrew, wickedly.

Poor Barbara was probably one of the smallest living
sheep. At about six months, she was little bigger than a
Yorkshire terrier and had more things wrong with her than
any other pet lamb I have ever dealt with, with the possible
exception of Snuff in her early days.

Matters were not helped by the fact that she had an
unsightly abscess at the base of one of her horns, and when I
had finished cauterising it with a de-horning iron and
shaving off all the soiled wool round her face to discourage
flies her poor head looked like a little black egg.

Her soft, Dalesbred wool wisped out round the fistful of
birdbones that passed for a body. She was the last lamb to be
weaned from the bottle and had had a scoop of extra food
every day since, but she still didn't seem to have grown a lot
since she came. Not so much your woolly lamb – more your
inexpertly-crocheted ferret. But oh, how we loved her.

The point is, though, that Barbara looked just like that
when we chose her and she was picked not in spite of it but
because of it. Nancy looked at a whole straw-penful of lambs
but had eyes only for Barbara, and it's no good laying the
blame on Nan, because I know I couldn't have left her behind, once I had seen the little mouse face looking up at me.

At last we heard the sound of a car door slamming, and out we rushed to see what we had drawn from the bran-tub this time. A strong, loud, healthy pig, without doubt, but it was almost dark and by the time her former owner had gone there was nothing to be seen but a bulge in the straw bedding that rose and fell with rhythmic sighs.

In the morning we raced to be first to see the new pig, but the queue had already formed. Magnus the Shetland pony stood nose to nose with her through the wire mesh and the goats filed up behind him for a sniff and a stare. She was obviously enjoying their attention immensely.

She was the most adorably ugly pig you could imagine, with random spots on her bum and an exploratory snout that thrust between the most majestic ears; silk purse material if ever I saw it. They flapped over her face to blot out what displeased her like the apron of an old-fashioned housekeeper, and the little eyes underneath were keen and bright.

The amazing thing was that she seemed to be everybody's idea of what a pig ought to look like and everyone agreed she was just what we wanted. We called her Rosalie.

In just seven days, Rosalie Pig became one of the Drysdales. I suppose it proved something, this immediate affinity with creatures so universally regarded as lacking in dignity and decency, but nothing, I dare swear, that most people didn't know already.

On that very first morning, when she stepped happily out of her sty and treated her new home to the benign smile that has since proved not only a part of her appearance but also of her personality, I knew she was Our Pig.

Playing cricket with Robert and happily taking on the rotten job — deep field in the nettle patch — running at full pig-power down the hill with Nancy to their mutual delight, digging in the potato patch for any that had been left behind or just coming to sit beside me while I drank my cup of tea on the front step, she was the very essence, the summing-up of my highest ideals of piggery.

She soon arranged her sty just the way she wanted it, and organised her sanitary arrangements with an outside lavatory in the bottom left-hand corner of her own private yard. No mess indoors. Each morning she spread her bedding boisterously as if she wanted to air it, and each night she gathered it all in the corner piling it into a great eminence like a termite hill and plunged herself underneath it to as great a depth as she felt necessary, according to the weather conditions. One morning when I went to see her, she rose like a spaceship from a great volcano of straw and toddled out to relieve herself in the appointed place. Before she came I had white-washed the lower third of her sty wall and, typically, left brush and whitening lying around. Someone added, above my demarcation line – 'Rosalie rules – O.K.?'

Toddy Pig-husband arrived one night in the back of a pick-up truck and he wasn't in the least what I had expected. The tailboard dropped down and out he stepped – the most enormous boar pig you ever did see. Like a great pink rhinoceros he strode out of the back of the truck and sailed like a galleon into Rosalie's accommodation. She let out an anguished shriek and ran. I can't say I blamed her.

We had known for a long time that we could not put off forever the delicate problem of finding Rosalie a mate so that she could fulfil the job nature designed her for and rear us some piglets as her contribution to the enterprise. I had been asking tentatively among my acquaintances for weeks but only finally plucked up courage to ask someone who could actually provide a boar as well as advice, in Northallerton Mart one Wednesday. Then everything moved with lightning speed and I was promised a suitable boar within a few days. Now I knew that a young gilt should be served by a smaller boar than the mature sow, who is better equipped to withstand heavyweight tactics. I imagined that the boar would be somewhere around the size of Rosalie herself, who was slightly bigger than the half-pigs you see hanging in high street butchers. I was wrong. What a monster!

I saw them standing together and worried. Surely boars didn't come much bigger than Toddy Pig-husband. I fetched a bale of straw and set to enlarging the nuptial bed to accommodate his great frame.

After a bit of perfunctory posterior-snuffling they both settled to an uneasy truce and I finished feeding the other creatures and went indoors. When I crept out later to see how they were, I found poor Rosalie sleeping in the concrete yard, while inside the building the great boar stretched out right in the middle of the warm, clean bed. Rosalie's bed. Suddenly I was very angry. What gave this visitor the right to take over the entire sleeping accommodation? Rosalie was always particularly fastidious about her bed, keeping it clean and dry and adjusting the amount of straw cover to the prevailing weather conditions. I had brought enough straw to make two beds and now here was this fellow hogging the lot! Hogging? I started to laugh. Toddy Pig-husband fixed me with one beady eye. The silliest thought had occurred to me and I prodded the great hulk wide awake. 'You,' I told him, 'are a real, live male chauvinist pig.' He sighed and went back to sleep.

I didn't think twice about moving him, although it was much easier said than done. I heaved his vast bulk over to one side, despite his total lack of co-operation, and hauled out a fair share of the bedding from under his great carcase. Then I called Rosalie and scratched her belly until she lay down on what I considered to be a fair share of the straw. But she was still uneasy, so I stayed there, scratching her belly with one hand and Toddy Pig-husband's bristly skull with the other. Two or three times I tried to get up and leave, but always Rosalie jumped up in fright. I stayed with my back propped against the sty wall, my eyelids drooping lower and lower until I woke with that sudden cold jolt that anyone who has ever fallen asleep where they shouldn't will know only too well. Both pigs were sighing gustily and their whiskery flanks rose and fell, slightly out of synchronisation. I crept stiffly out of the pigsty and back indoors to my own bed.

In the morning I showed T.P. to a neighbour, complaining that he was surely far too big for poor Rosalie. 'Why, that's nobbut a little 'un,' I was told. I was also told that I must take care when handling boar pigs. I must not attempt any familiarity and above all I must not turn my back on him. 'All right', I said, and swallowed hard. I had been going to recount the night's adventure, but I changed my mind.

The liaison, though, had its inevitable result. It was eight o'clock on a mild September evening and all was well. The only thing wrong was that it was a Wednesday, and according to my calculations, Rosalie's piglets should have been born the previous Sunday.

I wore my brain thin trying to spot where I had made the error in my calculations and returned every time to the impossible conclusion that she was overdue. Pigs, I was told, don't go over their time. I knew by heart all the signs of imminent farrowing listed in the impressive array of pig-keeping books on the shelf under the window. Maybe I should have kept them in the sty, I told myself gloomily, so that Rosalie could have read them too.

By now she should have been acting strangely, making a nest in her straw, oozing milk at the slightest touch and swelling visibly behind. None of these signs was present. I watched her constantly for strange behaviour, but it is rather difficult to spot strange behaviour in a pig as individual in her habits as Rosalie, since none of her preferred activities really came within the scope of the books I had to hand.

They're all very hot on Danish cage-rearing, three-week weaning and variations in food conversion ratios, but none of them give any practical advice on the main problems I have come up against, such as the reinforcing of doors. Not of her doors, to keep her in, so much as of my doors, to keep her out.

On the rare occasions that she managed to effect an entry into my more personal preserves, she has usually busied herself with the apparent necessity of piling all the furniture somewhere central to give her a clear space to stretch out and snore.

A few days previously I, and a neighbour's wife, had to re-hang a twelve-foot oak gate that she had lifted off the crooks and laid flat on the ground because it stood between her and where she wanted to be.

The neighbour himself found it hard to believe – not so much that we had managed to hang it, but that Rosalie had managed to unhang it in the first place. It seems that several times he had attempted to remove that gate to make it open the other way and had been quite unable to shift it.

The straw nest was another non-event. Rosalie always makes a nest. Never have I met an animal more economical in her use of straw. She will never wet or soil her sleeping-corner, and I still have no hesitation, in spare moments, in settling down beside her in straw that remains sweet and fresh week after week.

Nor was there any milk. A slight swelling of the udder, yes, but no actual milk. Every day I approached her udder with questing fingers and at my touch she would 'die for the Queen', grunting happily while I explored the possibility of its presence; but milk there was not.

On these occasions the children would come up, begging to be allowed to feel the piglets while Rosalie lay, apparently enjoying the touch of small cool hands as they learned through their fingertips the joyful squirming of the life within.

I noted the absence of any swelling and returned to my calendar to go over my arithmetic once more. But however I looked at it, Rosalie was well into borrowed time. So there it was, Wednesday, and there was still no real sign and our waiting was at an end. Just a sort of feeling.

I went out at ten and heard her grunting to herself. I crept in to look, and she leapt up from her nest expecting food. I went out at midnight and didn't open the door so as not to disturb her. I peered over the top and stretched my arm round the corner to direct the torch at Rosalie's sleeping form.

She snored and I went to bed. But I set the alarm for two, and went again. Still no piglets. At four she was still stretched out, apparently quite at peace, but now and then a great sigh would shake her bulging frame and I felt sure that she must at least be dreaming about farrowing.

I made myself a cup of tea, decided not to go back to bed, sat in the armchair and fell into the deep and tranquil sleep that only the would-be vigilant ever achieves.

Having messed about with the alarm clock all night, I hadn't set it back for its usual quarter-to-six and it was twenty past when the cockerel woke me. I ran to the sty. Fool, fool – I should never forgive myself if the poor pig needed my help and I had let her down . . .

At the door I stopped. A new noise came from within. A sort of soft, audible silence punctuated by a rhythmic, satisfied grunting. I opened the door very quietly – and there they were. Eight little pigs, beautifully fashioned from salmon-pink velvet, laid out on a cushion of golden straw, all plugged in to their source of nourishment and comfort.

There was no sign of the damp and grubby side of birth; Rosalie had taken care of all that. Only the little tableau of satisfaction and joy, only a sow and her litter. Just like my Mum's Aynsley Pottery sow which had always seemed such a good model – until now.

In the accumulated warm of the sty I stood and looked at my own little group and knew for sure that no human craftsman, however gifted, could catch and hold that perfect moment. Already it was slipping away. My own acceptance of the miracle was almost complete, and with the telling of the story to the first willing listener, it would be over.

I knelt down quietly and, with the end of my middle finger, touched the tiny domed skull of the littlest pig where the silver down stirred in the breath of its nearest sibling. Then I crept out, shut the door, and went to wake Nancy.

Those piglets grew from precious mites, hidden in deep

straw behind a closed door from the worst excesses of daytime weather and the inclement breath of the cold night air, to a collective tornado, a giddy eightsome reel, careering round corners and upsetting everything and each other in their enthusiasm for the great outdoors which is to them a paradise of hidden treasures which can be brought to light by the magic touch of their india-rubber noses.

Dear pigs, whose only problem seems to be the inability to agree as to which of life's delights should be sampled next, manifesting itself in their noisy gallops from the fallen plums at the back of the house to the mud-hole at the front.

Their boldness grew daily. They had been afraid of the very sound of the water running through the yard, but now they waded into it on all short fours, letting it ripple round their bellies as they drank, lifting their heads from time to time as though telling each other that this water, their water, was the finest in the world. I was suddenly reminded of my dear sister-in-law, a lady somehow larger than life, as she sat on the floor of friends' house, a little the worse for some celebration, singing at the top of her lungs 'Oh, Campbelltown Lock, I wish ye were whisky.' The pigs behaved as though the cool spring water which ran through their territory were something just as miraculous. I suppose, having tasted the water in cities all over England, they're right. This was only one of a number of things of whose wonder they reminded us as we shared in their daily voyage of discovery through things we had begun to take for granted.

At first, they followed closely behind their fond mother, squealing piteously if they felt themselves lost or left behind, showing me that the little pig of my babyhood, who cried 'wee wee wee' all the way home, was no figment of anyone's imagination. But now they took a fiendish delight in galloping off on their own to special secret places, finding their way unerringly back again just when you thought they must be lost forever.

When the time finally came for the cattle to have the last

precious fields of fog, Magnus the pony had to stay behind.
At first he was noisy, ill-tempered and lonely, but later in the
day he trudged miserably into the yard looking crestfallen,
and found, for the first time, the little pigs.

He was already a friend of Rosalie, grooming her as though
she were a horse companion while she grunted with pleasure
until he nipped too hard, but he had never before been in
anything like close contact with the little ones. I was afraid
the squealing crew, squirting higher and yon like bits of wet
soap, would frighten him so that he struck out, perhaps
injuring one of them in his panic. I needn't have worried.

He was delighted with them. He bent to sniff them and
they jumped and scuttled. He trotted gently round the yard
and they milled round his feet with the low murmur of noise
that sounds a bit like muffled giggling. He followed them
dutifully on their travels round the house, and finally followed them into the sty where they collapsed exhausted. I
went in behind him and he turned to look at me as if to say
'aren't those grand?'. I agreed with him.

The next day was the first on which they went far from
home without Rosalie. They disappeared completely.
Rosalie was sleeping unconcernedly in the sty and I feared for
their safety. I imagined them out on the road, run over and
killed. I imagined their little pink bodies bobbing down the
river. I ran from field to field, calling 'Pigs! pigs!' until it was
almost dark, and then I remembered Magnus.

I called his name and he answered. I ran to the alder copse
he called from, and there they were. It was like a picture from
Winnie-the-Pooh, with Magnus like a sad and gentle Eeyore,
legs splayed and head dropping while around him played, not
Piglet, but piglets. Eight little tearaways, sporting with
their new-found uncle until it was truly dark when they
returned with much demanding noise to their gruff and
grunting mother who had clearly enjoyed her bit of peace.

Since then I have accepted the fact that little pigs can take
care of themseleves.

After that first lot of pigs were sold and the seeds of the second lot sown, Rosalie continued to flourish. One day I was assisting at a sheep-dipping session in the handling pens that adjoin our yard, when one of the others present, who had not been at our house for some time, happened to look up as Rosalie stepped out into her enclosed yard for a stroll. 'Pig's grown,' he said.

Rosalie's yard was fastened shut by a gigantic 'stock-proof' bolt which prevented her from bumping the latch off its keeper and held the bottom of her heavy door fast against her occasional onslaughts of enthusiastic jailbreaking.

However, Rosalie was often allowed out for a trot, although only when I was on hand to see she didn't do any unscheduled demolition or mole-ploughing, both of which activities were hobbies of hers when she got bored with eating. I let her out myself one day while I cleaned out her sty, and she went out of sight behind the house to where the goats were eating up some stale Rice Krispies.

I can't have pulled the door really tight. Normally you can't open it without a key or a bank card (that's why they call them Access, I suppose!) but when I went round the back to see how they were getting on, I found three goats and an open door. I rushed inside and there she was, in the back kitchen as before, but what a difference; she seemed to fill all the available space and every movement of her great pink body shook something. I dived to save the crockery on the table and transferred it to the sink. She gurgled happily and cuddled up against me as I squeezed past her. 'Pigs!' I squealed, in the shrill call that summons her to me for food.

She was only too well aware, though, that all the food she could possibly want was in the row of bins along the wall. She went to the biggest and shouldered it. I dived again to stop it falling over. This was clearly a case for extreme measures. I snatched the lid off a jar of raspberry jam and waved it under her snout. When it had her undivided attention, I backed slowly towards the door. She followed ponderously and I spooned a generous dollop on to the flags while I sprinted to close the door.

What I couldn't get over was the vast size of our beloved pig against the little table, the big cornbin and the fridge, all of which had been in the same positions during her former escapade. She is now truly enormous. I am quite proud of her.

I was trying to explain my discovery to a neighbour who didn't seem at all delighted with the idea. She was quite horrified at the thought of a pig in a kitchen. 'What about the smell?' she asked. 'Oh,' I said airily, 'Rosalie didn't seem to notice it.'

Hatching Plots

'Mum', Andrew announced. 'There's a black hen sitting on a nest in the corner of the henhouse.'

'Andrew,' I said, 'We haven't got a black hen.'

It was several years ago that I got rather bored with the little black bantams that scurried like feathered ants about their eggy business and treated them to a series of different cockerels, each progressively lighter, until this latest generation are a veritable shade-card, like you see in decorators' shops, all possible permutations of speckles on varying shades of grey, with two real beauties in Brilliant White.

I have watched this transformation with mild delight, and it is a source of pride to me that we no longer have any black ones. Apart, that is, from old Black Beauty. And she couldn't possibly be sitting.

When we first came to live in the Dale, our near neighbour had some hens of a type I hadn't seen before — Arbor Acres — of which he was most anxious to be rid, since they were all of advanced years and erratic in production. Ugly birds they were, mainly black, but some tinged with gold around the neck, the only uniform feature being the evil amber eyes with which they glared malevolently on the world.

His daugher-in-law's mother had a deep-freeze, quite a novelty then, and the old dears were shipped en masse to his son's house, where they were to be slaughtered, plucked, and put in little plastic bags in preparation for a time of siege or whatever it is people freeze things for. What with one thing and another, it didn't get done straight away, and they fluttered around for a while, teasing the dogs and raiding the kitchen until the son, too, grew sick of the sight of them and did the fell deed in hot blood after some misdemeanour or other. However, by this time, nobody quite remembered how many there had been, and when the last squawk faded away and the last feather spiralled to the ground, a pair of cold beady eyes was watching from somewhere or other and Old Black Beauty lived to fight another day.

She was seen pottering about quite openly. Deposits of eggs were found among the hay-bales. Deposits of bird-droppings were found on the machinery and at last, one fatal day, the old girl herself was found in the back of the young man's Landrover.

Unfortunately, he had been off on a visit to his father, and when he opened the door she hopped out and sauntered off, to their mutual chagrin. I laughed like a drain when I heard the story. The father caught her and returned her to the son, who presented her to me, partly as a solution to their problem, and partly to show me what happens to people who laugh at other people's misfortunes. And she is still here.

Nobody really treats the venerable creature with the respect she deserves. My neighbour's daughter-in-law never asks if she is still alive, always 'Isn't she dead yet?' and when I tell people that she is still laying eggs for me, they say, 'Nay, she can't be.' But she is. Special eggs, they are, with two pointed ends; awkward as their mother, they wobble in every egg cup I have, but they are quite distinctive and undeniably hers.

For the past few years they have furnished my excuse for not despatching her to the bottom shelf of the oven where everybody says she belongs. I have a perverse desire to see just how long the feathered crone intends staying on this earth. And, strange as it may seem, I love her.

Arbor Acres are one of those strange breeds of hen, specially selected for their lack of the usual tendency to go broody. This Arbor Acre is over eleven years old. Therefore, it would seem extremely unlikely that the mysterious broody hen in the corner of the henhouse could be our Old Black Beauty. But as I went with Andrew to have a look, I hoped for a little miracle.

And I found one. With difficulty, as it turned out, since I constructed the henhouse out of the existing outside lavatory, purely as a place for night-roosting in security, and left only a small entrance at ground level. I had grown a bit of extra behind over the winter months and found myself utterly wedged at the widest point, head in the henhouse, feet sticking out, while Andrew howled with mirth and Old Black Beauty, for she indeed it was, pecked furiously at my left ear.

Weak with laughter, I lay flat on my back in the poultry manure. The old hen subsided, muttering, on her clutch, but not before I had seen that every one of them had two pointed ends.

Perhaps she knew in her flinty old heart that this was her last chance. I truly believe she did. Just as I knew with utter certainty that one of those eggs would contain a black pullet of uncertain temper, with beady amber eyes, and that I should keep her to the end.

With the first gales of winter came the arrival, safe and sound, of 17 guinea-babies, in assorted shades, hatched amid howling gales and hailstorms by the indefatigable Dodo. She ended her month's work-to-rule with a single-minded 72-hour sit-in, somehow generating enough heat in these impossible climatic conditions to hatch 17 of the 20 eggs she attempted.

Of the three remaining, only one was untenanted. The other two I hatched gently by hand but the two tiny occupants were dead. I assume that the gentler brooding of the 17 living chicks had created an environment too cool for the hatching of the latecomers. Certainly the eggs were colder when I took them from the nest than when I had surreptitiously turned them for her in her absence in the early days.

All through those last, long days, Archie, her mate, had sat beside the wire run which I had added to her coop when I knew the end was near. His whirring and chirruping must surely have encouraged her, as she slowly but surely accomplished what so many people had told me was quite impossible at that time of year. Now I had to help her to protect them against the cold, the wet, the wind. And from the Red Baron.

He came first on the night I gave Dodo the wooden coop. I was awakened in the early hours of the morning by the clamouring of the ducks, who always slept in a flock right under my bedroom window. I went out to see what was the matter, and carried them, wooden and staring, to the safety of a big wire pen, where I had once fastened the youngsters as protection from the jealousy of the senior drake. The dog had barked, but only once or twice. Only Archie, as I scuttled shivering indoors, kept up his terrible alarm call. I told myself he always was an old panic-monger and went back to sleep. It must have been the pet lambs blundering through on their way to shelter in the carthouse.

When it was light he had stopped his racket. There was a silence over everything that was somehow more profound than usual. Something was not quite right with the world. Even so, it was half-an-hour before I found the first of the dead hens, her head missing, so near to Dodo's coop that I had been unable to see it from the house. There were two more.

The obvious thing to do was to tell the gamekeeper, but I decided against it. No more drugged carrion. No more dead cats. The keeper came down later that day to take some corn to his pheasants and I said nothing, willing him not to look up the hill where the evidence still lay. A killer fox.

It was after this that I added the wire run to the coop, shuddering at how near disaster poor Dodo had come. I made a game of it — 'Archie versus the Red Baron' — and gloried in my secret. After all, I could shut up the poultry and Archie could always warn me when he was about.

How he must have shouted in the small hours of the morning after I had been to talk to the members of the Hampsthwaite Ladies' Circle. How they all must have cried out in the half-light. But I can't be sure because I wasn't there.

When I arrived back at the house where I had left the twins, the friends there had put them to bed, because I was so late back. I felt warm and grateful – and asked if I, too, might stay and hitchhike back when it got light.

So I did. And when I ran back down the hill to the house, the same cold silence was waiting for me.

Archie was huddled against Dodo's coop, whining quietly. The ducks waited silently in their yard. The sheet of tin was missing from the ground-level door of the henhut, the main door was still shut – but the whole front of the shelter, made from a sheet of heavy-duty polythene, was ripped from top to bottom. Something had torn its way out in terror. Something grey, I could see the feathers trailed all down the little pasture and the still heap at the bottom of the gill.

I wasn't in a hurry to know and I put off as long as possible the moment of certainty.

It was Cuckoo, the maran cockerel. A great, strong bird, he had put up a fight by the look of things. And his fine head was missing and his carcase was horribly mutilated.

The Red Baron had struck again. I laid plans to bring Dodo indoors.

Anyone brought up in my neck of the woods will tell you that there are 'forty farsand fevvers on a frush'. There are probably not quite as many on a guinea fowl's behind, but it must be well into treble figures.

I found that out when I embarked on the delicate operation of moving Dodo and her guinea-chicks to a place of greater safety and it was during this enterprise that I found myself stretched full-length in a wire run, on a surface as foul as only intensive poaching by poultry can make it, with chicks everywhere and Dodo nowhere and a huge handful of tail feathers to show for my ill-timed effort at grabbing her.

The day had begun oddly. I was awakened at first light by a gentle kiss. Nothing unusual in that for the more fortunate of us, but, as far as I remembered, I had been alone when I fell asleep. Again the gentle brushing of lips across my face, spiced by the unmistakable prick of whiskers. A prince, of course, and with a moustache. I lay a moment longer with my eyes closed convinced that, with my present run of luck, he would turn into a frog if I opened my eyes, but when the tentative caress gave way to a heavy breathing, I felt I had to peep.

At the same moment my visitor deemed it time to speak. A great cavernous bellow straight down my right earhole. Snuff. There I lay, staring up at her dear, daft grin, noticing through the mists of sleep that there were now four broad teeth adorning it. We're none of us getting any younger, I suppose, and I knew with grim certainty that being bawled awake by a sheep, even when it's a good friend, had put a few more silver threads among the gold, as you might say.

I really must buy a bolt for the front door. When the man came to put on a new one he had been given none of the usual fittings that go with it, so he had to make the old hinges do again, borrow the latch from the dairy and use the bolt from the ferret hutch to make all secure, and I had to try to make them last until my ship came in.

At that time, though, my ship was standing offshore, waiting for the spring tides, and the ferret-hutch bolt finally gave in for the last time to the visitor who, thinking the door was stuck, gave it 'a bit of knee' and it now was in no state to repel old Snuff, whose knobby skull gains her entry to the unlikeliest places. Like my bedroom. She had had to bump open two more doors to reach me and heaven knows how long she had been waiting for me to show signs of life. There was a neat pile of gleaming black currants in the corner of the fireplace. I dressed quickly and hurried her outside before she augmented it.

It was raining mournfully but with the dogged determination of a day-long downpour. With a sinking heart, I rushed to the run where Dodo and the babies were living, and my worst fears were realised. Another two lay dead in a pool of water at the entrance to the coop. One choked on whole wheat grains, one smothered, one trodden on in a panic and now two drowned. I had to take the risk of upsetting Dodo and move the whole issue to somewhere drier and less draughty. Only a dozen left.

I took the two little bodies for disposal and thanked my stars that I hadn't yielded to my daughter's whim and given them all names. I couldn't have coped with funerals for Muriel, Gavin, Tracy and Maud anyway, and when they're all milling about like tufty jumping beans, they're quite uncountable, so losses aren't quite so tragic. They have a fine collective name that suits them all. If you have ever seen the innocent faraway expression of a broody bird and then glanced beneath it and seen the unlikely assortment of tiny feet sticking out at all angles below her, you wouldn't need to ask the reason. We call them Legs and Co.

The real problem was getting them all into protective custody while I moved the coop and run into a handy building. I planned it like a war game.

Using a blanket, I would drive them all down to the end of the run. Then I would grab Dodo and put her in a box while I caught the little ones and gave them back to her. I could cover the box with the blanket while I shifted the happy home, and then put them all back in it. It was all automatic!

Using a blanket, I drove them all down to the end of the run. Then I grabbed Dodo. That was when things started to go wrong, because I missed her leg, got her tail and then she whizzed up and over my shoulder screaming something most unladylike and sat at a safe distance discoursing like a fishwife on the subject of human interference. Her entire tail was still in my hand.

Her mate, Archie, now took part, advising her in a chattering crescendo what to do next. I could have wept.

Instead I began to giggle uncontrollably and launched myself in a series of abandoned rugby tackles on top of the poor old girl as she fussed hither and yon, refusing to go with Archie and leave the babies, who were still fizzing behind their blanket.

I got her. But what to do with her? I had flattened my box. I dimly recall opening the rabbit hutch with my teeth, shoving Dodo in with one hand while hauling the rabbit out with the other, and then trailing the heavy run towards the building with 12 chicks in a sort of marsupial carrying bag made of folding up the front of my jersey. Archie followed at a safe distance, watching.

We finally gave in to Archie's doleful whistling and allowed him access to his 12 children, though I had reason to suspect we might have made a grave mistake. I went to chase him out and shut them up for the night, only to find that Dodo, his mate, only had four baby guinea fowl huddled beneath her scrawny breast. I imagined the worst. Eight little bodies, torn apart in a frenzy of jealousy or driven friendless from their home to unknown dangers. After a heartbroken search, they were finally found, safe and warm, in below Archie's paternal wings.

I had heard of cock birds taking a turn on the nest and have seen many of the smaller ones feeding nestlings with their beaks — but never brooding their young with the same tender solicitude as the female of the species. Was this, I wonder, a peculiarity of guinea fowl. Or was Archie just a particularly good father. On the other hand, perhaps he realised that the end of November was a strange time to hatch young ones and that Dodo was by now well advanced in moult and no longer up to her job.

It was the height of summer when I first saw Mammy's Army.

If anyone has ever pointed out to you a Khaki Campbell duck, you may well have wondered why such a name should be given to a gentle pale-brown bird. I wondered myself until the morning when I saw for the first time a detachment of day-old ducklings, and then I was prepared to acknowledge the accuracy of the description.

Just as the Drysdales were all at sixes and sevens, about to depart for the Summer Games, into the yard walked Mammy, trying to look as though she was unaware of our obvious delight, followed by half-a-dozen of the little darlings and they were truly the strangest colour — not brown, not green, not yellow but a sort of amalgam of them all, and it amazed me profoundly that nature should have selected her yukkiest colour for something so delightful as a baby duck.

In a flash I was transported to the top deck of a bus travelling down Princes Street in Edinburgh, desperately trying to make conversation with my new mother-in-law. As we halted by the window of one of those old-fashioned stores I saw inside it the most hideous garment I had ever laid eyes upon. I can't remember now what it was or what it looked like, but I know that I drew mother-in-law's attention to it by way of a conversation piece. I said I loathed it. She stared hard through the window of the stationary bus and finally delivered her own opinion. 'It would be quite nice, dear,' she said, 'for the person it would suit.' There was no answer to that.

Looking at those ducklings, though, I somehow saw what she might have meant. On them it didn't look half bad, when you got used to it.

Mammy led the brood into the yard, clucking encouragement as they flung themselves over the huge four-inch timber that formed the bottom of the gate. Suddenly they were not ducklings any more but awkward little soldiers — raw recruits, perhaps, picking their way tentatively round a great assault course, walking sore-footedly in new boots. They were no ordinary ducklings. Not surprisingly, since Mammy is no ordinary hen.

I can't quite remember how old she is. She was hatched from a surprise clutch of mixed eggs given to a young friend of mine, who gave me all the chicks when neighbours threatened to shoot them for trespassing in their vegetable gardens. She is a fat little bantam, speckled with assorted colours on a beige background, like scotch broth. She has sky-blue patches on her cheeks and feathered feet like a vulture.

Her greatest claim to fame, though, was her mammoth sit-in all one summer on five medium-sized onions. I had given her back to my young friend Caroline to hatch some eggs from her own ducks, a task which she accomplished perfectly, but when the ducklings were grown, she started to lay again on a shelf in the back porch. However, the shelf sloped just enough to let each egg slide to the concrete below so Mammy, undaunted, moved herself onto a box of greengrocery further along the shelf and solemnly brooded her five onions for seven weeks, until I relieved her by sending Caroline a few real eggs just on the point of hatching which we slid under Mammy, stealing her onions one by one. She reared these chicks to maturity and then, when Caroline's family went to America, she came home again to live with us, still bearing her proud reputation of having never lost a single hatchling.

Her place in the pecking order of the yard fowls is in some doubt as she considers herself apart from them. She is always first in the house each morning and if I close the top half of the door against her she creeps through the broken window. She allows herself to be picked up and stroked and eats with expertise from a spoon, a fork or a finger. Nancy suggested lending her to her friend, Tracy, who needed a parrot for the fancy dress parade, but someone found a plastic one. Just as well, really, because on Summer Games day, our Mammy was otherwise engaged.

I had given her the six deserted duck eggs just to keep her sitting, and I intended slipping her some of her own grand-chickens, due to hatch later in the week. I never thought she could hatch the poor, cold foundlings, especially as she seemed to spend so much of her time sitting on the draining board talking to me.

But there they were in the yard that summer morning, six little soldiers, their legs going nineteen to the dozen as though they were painted-on wheels rotating below their fat, fuzzy bellies. Very beautiful; very khaki.

Ducklings, though, are not always easy to deal with. I remember one day when all was peace, relatively speaking. Nancy and I were collapsing in the easy chairs while upstairs Robert played his way through a selection of early Beatles hits that Andrew had passed on to him. It had been an extraordinary morning, but as we sat and supped greedily at the day's first wonderful cup of tea, it seemed hardly possible that only a short while before we had been engaged in a major civil engineering project, digging against the clock as though our lives depended on it, diverting the course of the stream that runs through the yard.

Mind you, it wasn't exactly our lives that had depended on it. It was those of two of the adjectival ducklings whose sole aim in life appears to be to perish violently before their fuzz turns to feathers and they outgrow such pretty pastimes.

We had watched over this breed of ducklings since they were laid, some on top of a pile of straw bales, some under a wall in a meadow, some, beautifully camouflaged, in the ruins of a derelict building adjoining the house. We watched as they neared hatching, and then collared most of the chipped eggs and gave them to trusted hens, having learned by sad experience that ducks, while doting mothers, are also somewhat dotty, expecting a degree of self-reliance and homing instinct in their offspring that is far in excess of their fuzzy capabilities, resulting in a sadly small number of ducklings reared in relation to eggs hatched. We left each duck one or two, to reward her for her persistence, and spirited the others off to a beautiful home-made run with two shelters and two reliable old broodies. Great.

The only trouble was, both hens wanted all the babies, and one was nearly killed before I gave in and rescued her, and within a few days the little devils had found a way to weasel under the wire of their pen and go adventuring. In the course of the week their numbers altered. Not diminished, mark you, but altered. They somehow managed to recruit the ducklings we had left with the ducks, who didn't seem to miss them unduly, so we ended up with twenty little fuzzy-wuzzies, in assorted shades from pale primrose to jet black and every last one of them hellbent on mischief.

What had happened on that particular morning was that I had attempted to move their run into a piece of clean ground without first assembling all the available force to ensure safe transit of the ducklings. They got out.

That, mind you, is the understatement of the season. They burst out, squeaking and scurrying in all directions at once like refugees from a police raid. Capture was inevitable, but they were damned if they were going to give up easily.

Up the field they sped, between the feet of the assembled cattle and escaping death by inches at each shift of the great hooves. They fell over their own flat feet and squealed on their backs in hollows, helpless. They ran themselves to a standstill in the long grass; but the boldest of them all dived into the stream that runs through the yard and bobbed like delighted corks on the broad, shallow water. They couldn't see the danger of the open mouth waiting to swallow them, the murky entrance to the concrete pipe that takes the stream under tarmac drive, and I raced to scoop them to safety before it was too late.

But for two of them, I wasn't quick enough. Their little legs just weren't strong enough to paddle against the current that drew them inexorably down into the depths of the great, black tunnel. I went cold; the horror of it was almost too great to comprehend. My babies had gone down the plug-hole, and I would never see them again.

I ran first to the other end of the pipe, but there was no sign of them. I came forlornly back to the place where they went in, and I heard them cheeping. I went for the torch and lay on my stomach, peering down the pipe. There they were, fetched up short by Robert's missing football, but were unable to make their way back to the entrance because of the swirl of water that was coming down. What could I do?

I remembered the old, inefficient stone drain that had taken the water away before the new pipe was installed. I found and unblocked its entrance. I diverted the water along it temporarily and then peered again down the dark empty pipe. They squeaked delightedly and scampered about, discovering that the green, slimy surface of the pipe contained a thousand duckish delights and they intended to sample them all before coming back to daylight.

Nancy came to join me and together we watched as the pair disported themselves in their new playground. Their little leathery feet made huge echoes as they slapped up and down and all we could do was wait until they had tired of the game and snaffle them as they came out.

Back in the house, I drank my tea and made a note of the jobs for the rest of the day. Borrow some drain-rods and retrieve that football. Put the water back where it belonged. Make a grating for the end of the pipe, but first check all the unevennesses of the new ground on which I had placed the run, so as to block up the escape routes.

Too late. Robert's voice echoed down the stairs. He had been watching from the upstairs window and now raised the alarm – 'Ducks out!'

'Shall I get them back?' asked Nancy. 'You'd better,' I

said. 'I might just wring their little necks.'

It hardly seems possible that those tiny adventurers became smooth-feathered, flat-footed young waterfowl, and went to new homes. We had done all we could for them and were already concentrating on the next lot of baby ducks which hatched out a few days before they went.

They, too, had rather an adventurous start in life. Their two mothers sat happily for three weeks on two separate nests, a yard apart, on top of a heap of straw bales. Then, suddenly, as their sit-in drew to a close, they decided to pool their resources and wheeled all the eggs to a central point and sat side-by-side like some two-headed heraldic hen, hissing at allcomers. The only trouble was, the place they had chosen to do it was over a crack between two bales, and several of the eggs slipped down, as did many of the ducklings and only an investigation of their anguished cries showed me what was happening.

Rescuing them was hazardous indeed. The two ducks, quite unaware that I had their interests at heart, and seeing me only as a nest-robber, attacked with everything they had, and in the case of a full-grown duck, that's quite a lot. My forearms, with which I had attempted to protect my face, were covered with black little bruises, and the angry creatures pulled out beakfuls of hair as I stuffed one after another of the icy little fluffballs down the front of my jersey. At last, when I believed that I had them all, I went into the house to lick my wounds and warm my ducklings.

My intention, at the time, was to restore some semblance of life to the frozen few, then return them to bosoms of their mothers, after having coaxed the latter to a place more conducive to the safe management of their ducklings. No chance. By the time I crept out again with a pinny-ful of joyful little squeakers, the ducks had utterly disappeared, lost without trace in the surrounding sea of soft, waving grass. All was silence.

I later discovered that the silly old pair had found one

single duckling that I had overlooked and gone off with it, sharing it amicably between them. They were a funny sight. The hen with one chicken has rightly become a symbol of the over-indulgent mother, but the two ducks with one duckling had to be seen to be believed.

Meanwhile, the problem of what to do with the ten survivors. Nancy had for some time been worrying over which of the first batch of ducklings she should choose for herself. She had been a great help in looking after them so it seemed the best way of rewarding her, and I told her she could choose two for her own. She loved the lame one until it got better and was indistinguishable once more, and she loved the two white ones, but they turned out to be drakes. So I borrowed a heat lamp from a neighbour and gave her these tiny ten, all for her own. She was overjoyed.

Next day I made her a cat-proof brooder for them with two old drawers hinged together, and she tended them scrupulously, changing their newspaper carpet several times a day and fussing over their food and water as though they were some exotic fowl worth thousands. She assumed full responsibility.

Spring slid into summer all unnoticed yet again. The little goats grew fit and strong, and young Pipsqueak the pet lamb and his boon companion, Blue, became quite independent, returning to the doorstep only for the occasional feed of milk and even that now was an indulgence rather than a necessity.

One day I received back in the post the prints of two films I took between the last autumn and early spring. We had only just saved up enough to have them done and get two more films for that summer. There they were again, Rosalie's first litter of piglets, guzzling plums under the trees. Gertie the goat, all slim and sleek, ready for the billy; Lazarus the sheep coyly encouraging the attentions of Harry, the fine Swaledale tup, and there too, incredibly, was Snuff, seated in queenly fashion in a snow-covered yard with three puny lambkins huddled against her cushiony fleece. To see them now –

Milly, Molly and Mandy, you would be hard put to it to accustom yourself to the idea that they were the same lambs. Now that Snuff was shorn and their coats had grown, they dwarfed her, even knocking her over sometimes in their rumbling, tumbling play.

One year we tried a few goose eggs. Snow White the hen settled herself patiently for a month on four great beauties, in the nest she had used three times already that year with no success. The trouble was rats.

She had chosen to nest in the corner of the barn, among a heap of ancient rubbish, and her first attempt at hatching here had ended in disaster on the very day the babies – ducklings they were – had been due to appear. I had my usual grope underneath to see how things were going on, and found that they were not going, but gone.

Not a trace of an egg remained, not a foot or a wing or a piece of broken shell. Rats.

Her second try failed when the young goats broke through the barrier I had built round her and danced on her eggs. Sadly Snow White returned to the yard for a while, then began to lay another clutch in the same ill-fated place. This time it was I who spoilt things: I moved the eggs to a place I considered more suitable. Snow White, though, held her ground as you might say. She continued to sit in the corner of the barn among the bits of turnip-chopper and rolls of rusty wire, although her eggs were now in a tomato box on the granary floor. Thus, when I was given a few goose eggs, I could not, in all conscience, deny Snow White her chance, and slipped them under the grateful little bird in the nest she still maintained desperately was the only place fit for chickens. But with a difference.

Do you remember the days of the gondola basket? They were part of the peripheral accoutrements of the fifties mod. They went with beehive hairstyles, winkle-picker shoes and the like, but everyone seems to have forgotten them now. I can remember going to work on the tube in London, standing room only, feet trampled to an agonised pulp from being stepped on by the sharp little heels fashion decreed, and the rest of my body buffeted by the ubiquitous baskets, in which every modern miss worthy of the name carried her white lipstick, black eyeliner and spare stockings, for the great bristly baskets were, as The Bard would have put it, a sore ladderer of your whoreson nylon stocking. This was well before the days of tights, so the afflicted could replace one stocking at a time, but still the gondola remained a fearful weapon, especially in the evening rush hours when it returned home filled with lunch-hour purchases.

Lurking on the top shelf of the old dairy was just such a basket. Retired now from public life and resting with a cargo of moletraps, it was, for the first time in its ungainly life, just what I needed.

I emptied out the moletraps, took a handful of straw and made a nest in it, laid my four precious goose eggs inside, and went to the corner of the barn. I lifted the muttering hen gently into the basket and asked her if she thought it was a good idea. She did.

When it was time for the eggs to hatch I went daily. First came the sort of taut, shiny appearance of the eggs themselves that I have come to recognise as a sign of impending chipping, then the sound of movement within the eggs, which told me there was a live gosling in each egg. Then the first bulging of the shell as though someone within had fired an airgun pellet. This was the stage at which those first ducklings had died, and I kept a close watch.

The first live gosling was there almost at once. Far too soon. Its little belly was too soft and fragile and it was bleeding badly. I took it and placed it under the borrowed lamp which had reared Nancy's ducklings a week or so before, and did my best, but it was hopeless. I removed the bits of broken shell and hoped for better luck with the rest, but still it puzzled me how the gosling had been born so roughly and so soon.

The next morning I went to the nest and slid my hand under Snow White. She purred softly and did not protest. What a gentle little hen, I thought to myself. I could see grey fur on her far side, and assumed it was a new gosling. My fingers touched it, feeling in the gloom the soft fur, the stalky legs, and then, even as I felt with my fingertips, the roughness of the sharp, skinny feet and the long, long tail. A rat.

A great, gravid female, it slid nonchalantly out from its hiding place and crept, without haste, over the edge of the basket and disappeared. Snow White purred. She didn't seem to have noticed. There was a great deal more blood in the nest and I was sure that the rat had almost completed her wicked work before I got there, but I lifted the gondola basket with all its precious contents and took it into the house. An inspection showed three live goslings, but they were weak and premature and all I could do was leave things to Snow White.

She managed. She didn't seem to mind their nasty green-yellow colour or their very strange appearance. These were the babies she had waited all year for and she was making the most of them. I returned the gondola basket to the dairy shelf.

We wanted names for the babies and suggestions were many. The children, for a bit of daftness, were saying that the names we chose must fit their surname, and asked me what it was: 'Goose, of course,' I said, laughing. 'Fred Goose', 'Horace Goose'. 'But we don't know if they're girls or boys.' 'Evelyn Goose, then.'

In the end, we called them Brent, Bean and Barnacle.

I don't like geese. Full-grown geese go about as though they were wearing jackboots and the males of the species in particular display a degree of chauvinism that I find upsetting. Geese don't like me, either.

For the first few days their little hen-mother brooded them

tenderly, but when they got too big for such foolishness and started to sleep alongside her instead, she decided to fly up to her perch at night, leaving them in a downy heap at the bottom. It was a day or two before I discovered this, and the tragedy occurred because the rats found out just one night earlier than I did. The result was what you might have expected – one dead, one mutilated, and poor lost, lonely Bean piping sorrowfully to his two brothers who wouldn't come out to play at chasing chickens, not ever again.

So much for the fortune at Christmas. So much for the fine Chinese geese filing past the window. Now there was only Bean, and the strangest thing happened.

I, who hated geese, became extraordinarily fond of Bean, and the rest of the family worshipped at his flat, leathery feet. Perhaps one goose, just by itself, wouldn't be a nuisance – already I saw the danger signals and I knew we were hooked. Unless he blotted his copy book severely or appeared un-happy, Bean would stay.

He had the life of Reilly. He spent his days outside, pottering with his mother, and his nights in a special box with us. He seemed to enjoy being carted about by the children and was most often to be seen sticking out from under someone's arm, his legs dangling like the peripheral parts of a set of bagpipes. He submitted to being measured for a rather fetching striped jersey, but it proved impossible to get the armholes in the right places and it rode up round his neck when he strode off to look at himself in the pond. He neither squawked nor pecked, his only comment being a sustained and cheerful whistling. He was, all in all, a pleasant-natured bird.

He had obviously not yet attained his full potential, but it was most interesting to watch him develop. He seemed all disjointed and ill-put-together, his legs projecting from his sides as though they were put on afterwards, with pins. His head seemed too heavy, so that it tipped forward as he went along and he had to run to keep up with it and the down that made him feel warm as toast when you held him against your cheek and trembled like thistledown when you blew into it gave, as yet, no indication of what he would become.

Like a real craftsman-built thriller, whose story-lines seem to bear no relation one to another until the last pages, our Bean was a collection of apparently unconnected components all poised and waiting to come together into an integrated goose, I hoped.

That was really my only worry. We all called Bean 'him' because it was impossible to attribute such characteristics as this funny little creature had to anything female, but still I clung to the hope that, at the end of this happy adolescence, waited a goose and not a gander.

I've stopped remembering about Henry, the chinese gander who nipped over half the buttocks in Osmotherley in his heyday, stopped thinking of pots of grease and continental quilts. I think now of the trusty geese who saved Rome and how a large responsible bird in the henhouse might give those wicked rats something to think about. I was converted; now it was up to Bean.

Seasonal Pursuits

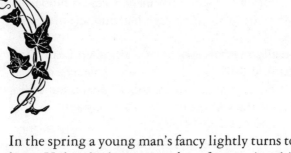

In the spring a young man's fancy lightly turns to thoughts of love. Unless he happens to be a farmer, in which case he is likely to be more concerned with the results thereof. Spring, for him, is one long birthday.

A typical spring, taken at random from a storehouse of happy memories, began, as always, with the nation's half-hearted tampering with its clocks while the temperature remained resolutely low. At about two o'clock in the afternoon, a single duckling flopped forth into the waiting world. When, after twelve hours, no other eggs had hatched, I decided to take over the care of the little harbinger of brighter days while his foster-mother sat a little longer, just to make sure. So into a shoebox on top of the paraffin heater went the adorable Donny, his fledgling fuzz gleaming like melted butter and his bugle-bead eyes peeping from under his woolly blanket to see where the next helping of porridge oats or muesli (with the raisins carefully picked out) was coming from. I was in the grip of a very heavy cold, which no doubt accounts for my rather jaded view of the proceedings, and coughed and spluttered my way through his formative days until, by the middle of the week, I had only to clear my throat within earshot of the shoebox for a veritable concerto of excited twitterings to begin, and these would mount to an inspired crescendo as I lifted the corner of the blanket and peeped in.

He would then climb happily into my hand and plod up my arm on damp, scaly feet to nestle against my ear, muttering 'cheep, cheep'. I would then extract him from my hair and glower at him with as much hardness of heart as any human can muster when confronted with one of nature's most lovable creations, and ask him to refrain from using the word 'cheep'. Penny for penny, as I pointed out to him, he must be about the most expensive piece of livestock on the place.

After three days I returned him to Bridget the Bantam with apologies for asking her to sit on the rest of the clutch for so long. Not one of them contained another duckling; Donny was to remain an only child. But never was one better loved, and he thrived under Bridget and her expert care.

Then the first of the kids arrived. Little black Laura was safely delivered of two little black babies and suddenly spring seemed to be getting underway again as they struggled gamely to their feet and made unerringly for the teats, all legs and ears and appetite.

While I was keeping an eye on Laura, I sent the other goats out to forage, so her middle-aged mother did not see or hear the little ones until her return to the shed. At first she stayed outside in the yard but gradually curiosity overcame her and she went in. On my last evening visit to check them all I found her muttering critically as Laura suckled them in the way of all grandmothers who feel overshadowed by their daughters' triumphs and launch themselves into a full-scale fault-finding mission. The following morning saw Laura out in the yard while old Bobo stayed indoors with her grandchildren. She was dozing when I peeped round the corner, her nose pressed between the two little bodies, while every now and then her great pregnant form was shaken by a deep, longing sigh. By mid-morning, the wishful thinking had possessed her utterly, and Laura's whimpers called me to the shed where her youngsters were being licked furiously by

Bobo, who seemed to have lost all memory of whose they were and how long they had been born. She was even using the growling, staccato speech of the new mother in her first communication with her young ones. She was nosing against them, urging them to suckle, in the total preoccupation that normally follows the delivery of the young goats or sheep and which, when it is misapplied by a pregnant animal to another's young, causes the weird phenomenon of spontaneous adoption — the lamb-thieving that can cause riot in a field of lambing sheep. It was interesting to observe it at close quarters and it taught me a great deal about something I have watched in other years among the neighbouring sheep without fully understanding the causes. Bobo muttered to Laura's kids for over an hour and at the end of that time she rolled her eyes heavenward in the vacant stare of one totally absorbed with the matter in hand that heralds the final effort of birth. Then, suddenly, a third little black kid made its appearance and she licked it joyfully into life, pausing only to return every now and then to her adopted pair who received the occasional lick apiece in the overspilling of her unleashed maternal drive.

This jolting out of phase of the natural succession of events leading to birth seems to be a particular hazard with sheep and goats. In the fields around the house, when the hill sheep come in to lamb, I have often seen dramas taking place that have turned a quiet corner of the hazel spinney into an action replay of the battle of Waterloo. Two old ewes may take the same corner for their lambing place. One may lamb before the other and the second will sometimes fight bitterly for the other's lamb in her growing desire for motherhood. As soon as her own lamb is born, the battle subsides, but while it lasts it is terrible to see.

Sometimes there are casualties. I have seen a young sheep lamb twins, the first cleaned and mothered by an older ewe during the first stage of her own labour. The old lady lost interest in her adopted lamb as soon as her own came, but by then the young sheep had trotted off with her second twin quite oblivious of the existence of the other little one who stayed lost and hungry till nightfall, when the shepherd applied his experience to the matter and ensured a happy ending.

Other variations on the theme can also occur. Perhaps a ewe will be so besotted with her adopted lamb that she leaves her own unlicked and unsuckled, thus creating an orphan lamb and a bereaved ewe through no fault of either of them. The shepherd is then faced with the choice of taking the stolen lamb from the thieving ewe and presenting her with a strange lamb that she neither knows nor wants, or giving the abandoned lamb to the bereft ewe, although it is not strictly her own. The latter seems to me the happier course — bringing together two creatures in need, as it were, rather than separating two happy and settled ones to cement a blood tie that is obviously already severed beyond all but a botched repair. Childcare authorities would do well, perhaps, to use a shepherd's skill rather than a genealogist's notebook.

This apparently perverted baby-swapping seems only to take place when the animals bring forth their young in closer proximity to one another than nature would normally permit. The housed goats, for example, had been denied the solitude that the free-ranging creature would find for herself, and the sheep, brought down from the moor, are forced closer together than would have been the case had they stayed on the common. It is as though, while the stages of physical labour progress in the appointed sequence, the emotional progress is hurried forward by the sight and sound, or even the taste and smell (how often a ewe will lick the spilled waters of another) of an accomplished birth.

So it was with Bobo, although soon things settled down to a sort of kibbutz arrangement with neither mothers nor kids bothering who suckled whom.

It was in the midst of old Bobo's lightning delivery that the dustman arrived. He had been promised the pick of

Laura's kids and chose the little, day-old Rose, who was subsequently weaned onto milk powder and made ready for human adoption. So delighted was he with his acquisition that I did not have time to examine Bobo's second kid until the excitement had died down. A huge ginger nanny with hair like picture-postcard sand and sharp blue eyes and knobby knees. I called her Googie. The only other person I have ever known with hair that exact unlikely shade was a girl in the East Anglian village where I spent my childhood summers. Googie, who showed me how to make fortunes from pop bottles dug from the local dump. Who lived on bubblegum from the American airmen on the base. Who later became queen of the Haverhill brush factory before toppling into marriage and maternity, though not necessarily in that order, with the same devil-may-care gusto with which she attacked all country matters.

It is now more than twenty years since she and I sat up in the branches of the hollow elm in Mr Willet's meadow, and she told me the secret of how babies are made and how they are brought forth and reared. I listened with the amazed deference that she had come to expect of me. But I didn't believe a word.

Amazing how springs invariably slide into summers and how seldom you actually see it happen. When I am riding in a car, and all the numbers in the middle of the speedometer are due to change, nine after nine of them into nought after nought, I always try to focus my concentration on them to the exclusion of all else until I have seen them all slide up and knowing that if I miss it I will have to wait for a long time before I get the chance to see it again, and yet a moment's inattention more often than not robs me of the sight of the actual change. So it is with the subtle sliding of spring into summer. Spring slips away unnoticed and is not missed until I look up from some routine job and see the grass rippling in the noonday silence that is the hallmark of summer, and all at once the summer tasks step forward from the horizon of happy anticipation and become pressing. The heady scent of late May blossom draws the bees in the light evenings and the moon daisies twinkle in the meadows. Everything is secret and hidden behind curtains of impenetrable green, and the limpid and lonely days are beginning again as the farmers send their tractors fussing like beetles to tidy up the loose ends before haytime, which grows ever nearer like a gathering storm.

Haytimes are either good or bad, judged on the speed with which they are concluded and the quality of the end result. This, in turn, is governed entirely by the weather. With typical perverseness, dry weather is not always welcomed unreservedly, especially at the beginning of summer. One haytime came, I remember, almost unexpectedly in just such a spell.

Around mid-June, the prayers for rain rose daily with the smoke of the newly lit fires, and the grass thirsted and grew grudgingly. New seeds lay discouragingly doggo among the sahara dust of the upland fields and the green shoots frizzled quietly around the edges of the corn. The pastures showed mysterious patches of scalded brown where stones beneath the surface denied the roots access to the deeper moisture and the dry quiet was broken only by sounds of half-hearted tinkering behind carthouse doors. The hay wasn't really ready, even if the weather was; just one good day's rain . . . but it didn't come.

In more usual years, grass grows longer and tempers grow shorter and as it ripens into seed each man watches his neights like other runners in a race, crouching on an invisible block, and woe to the ill-advised neighbour who asks brightly 'When are you going to start haytime?' One can only listen for the sharpening of mower knives and bear patiently with the agony of indecision.

That year, though, it became suddenly obvious to all that no further growth was possible, and to a man they bowed to the inevitable and laid low the parched acres, which yielded none too badly despite early misgivings. And in those last perfect June days the fragrant crop was bundled with sweat and good humour through its varied stages until it reached that most uninspiring of recent innovations – the bale.

It was then, as I gingerly flexed muscles dormant since last haytime and set to give a hand heaping, leading and stacking with my neighbours, that I realised the other implication of this burst of heaven-sent good weather. Never, in the past few years, had so many bales been handled so often by so few in such a short time.

The previous year as I stacked bales gamely with another volunteer we had worked one each side of the same bay in a dutch barn. After about five courses, perfectly worked out, carefully tied in, we met briefly in the middle and discovered that there was a rift between us, due to our polite refraining from overlapping one another's territory, that ran right to the bottom of the stack. While we waited for the gaffer to come and show us how to sort it out, he lamented the lost days of the haywain and handfork and in the next breath pointed out how much easier it would be if only the bales could be made of exactly equal size, each one half as broad as it was long.

After hefting something in the region of three thousand of the great monsters, I could see what he meant, although in thoughtful moments I still believed that the little individualities of bales maintain a link with those far-off days that would be lost altogether if things were more straightforward. There is a feeling of pride in adjusting one's technique to the bales available. A gentle lift for the shaggy ones, a knee in the right place for the bent ones and a karate-style 'Hai' for the big ones from the edges of the fields.

There is variety, too, in the industrial injuries sustained according to the constituents of the bale. The fragrant bits among old land hay, so relished by sheep in winter, work their way unerringly to the more intimate corners of the human frame and fidget there, mocking. Seed hay rasps the forearms with demon spikes and makes disaster areas of the knees until it requires a huge effort of will-power to submerge them in the bathwater. Ryegrass, worst of all, asserts its independence and wriggles free at the corners, bringing down the wrath of the man in charge and showers of loose hay and doubtful language from the top of the elevator.

But how intolerable if they were all alike. A man is no better than a machine without the chance to yell 'There's a hole here, send up a little 'un' or 'Put the big buggers round the outside.' Up they all go, each into his place, and there's still room for judgment and a little basic skill, as well as sweat and determination. But nevertheless it is pleasant when the elevator is finally silenced and the workers fall in a heap against the bottom of the stack. Oh, gaffer, when the day is over don't send me home — just draw the corner of the tarpaulin over me and send for the stackers' knackers.

Not all haytimes, however, gallop their course with such certainty. I remember the year I treated myself to a pair of special gloves for handling bales. Great blue-grey gloves made, so ran the label, of genuine horse hide. I bought them at Christmas from a gardening catalogue and broke them in on one glorious day in early July, the like of which did not occur again until September. Weeks later the swathes still lay in the meadows round the house, and a keen, cold wind drove the relentless drizzle against the window pane.

One day, a little less miserable than its fellows, I donned my gloves and joined the other members of the team, mustered outside ready to tie up the next field in line and the whole attempt ended in an undignified scurry for shelter as the weather finally made up its mind and rained. Everyone else went wistfully home as soon as was practicable, leaving me to wander back across the fields feeling fat, white and unloved, with the great gloves dangling like Minnie-Mouse paws, limp at the ends of my arms.

Back in the house, off with the gloves, dropping them with a wooden clatter on the kitchen table to lie like severed hands all cold and rigid. They looked unutterably silly. I poured a second flush of water onto my teabag and considered. The gloves lay idle on the table. I considered the literary trick whereby the elements reflect the human mood — pathetic fallacy it's called — and wondered whether it was still fallacy, albeit equally pathetic, when the state of the weather alters the human mood. But, like the chicken and the egg, the answer is immaterial. It is the masochistic pleasure afforded by attention to the problem which comforts, like the gentle probing of a hollow tooth with a sympathetic tongue.

I finished my cup of tea and went outside to stare about me. Black clouds or blue sky? I watched as my goats filed solemnly down the field between the rows. I wondered how many of them would have to be sold if the winter fodder situation grew really tight. I looked again at the lowering sky. Hay today or hay tomorrow? I was wearing my gloves, just in case, with my answer ready if anyone wanted a reason:

> When the grass is wet as window-cloth
> And the farmers pig-sick to a man,
> I would rather walk through the fields in gloves,
> Missing as much as I can.

Summer is also the season for sheep-shearing. The rising of both the sun and the lark have long been a literary inspiration. The rising of the sap brings with it a certain excitement and some degree of pleasant hazard. But here the second half of summer is the time for the rising of the wool on the backs of the hill sheep and for me that brings with it a keen anticipation of the pleasures of clipping time, together with the prospect of earning something, in cash or kind, towards the upkeep of my own tiny enterprise. This rise in the wool has a variety of scientific explanations, mostly concerned with increased secretion by the sheep's sweat glands, but this uninspiring piece of bodily chemistry has an effect that is beautiful to anyone who loves sheep. Between the grimy, matted winter fleece and the sheep's skin there appears a band of new, white wool, clean and untangled, which simply invites the shears, and through which they bite with a rhythmic ringing of steel until the whole fleece falls, bedewed with grease on its outside surface, to be flicked aside by the shearer's foot as he sends the sheep on her way and reaches for another.

Machine clipping is not as satisfying, especially the first few fleeces of the first day which seem to drop grudgingly with a fine shower of double-cut whiskers, but as the operators get into the swing of the job the fleeces fall quicker and cleaner and the catcher works harder as the sheep in the pen get fewer and dodge faster. An assistant steps in as each fleece falls and rolls it ready for packing. At first this was my job. The fleece is laid skin side down on a clean surface, loose debris picked off and soiled wool removed from the tail end. The two sides are folded to the middle and the whole thing rolled up towards the neck, the loose ends being pulled gently into a long strand which is lightly twisted into a cord to tie the finished bundle. It sounds simple, but you would hardly believe how a fine springy fleece takes on a mind of its own, especially towards the end of a long day, and how knees and elbows become bruised and calloused dealing with one of nature's softest commodities.

As time went on, though, the wrapping of the wool became something of a bone of contention, the other women of the dale suddenly claiming this job as a privilege in an upsurge of resentment that culminated in one of them instructing her menfolk not to 'tell Her where we're clipping' and Her, who knows such things by instinct, turning up anyway and nearly precipitating violence. So the next year, I stepped into the catching-fold, where no one else wanted to be, and worked there for my own flock, which had just become a reality with half a dozen good pet lambs to sell and four Swaledale gimmers promised at weaning time.

The following year there was a special joy as the sheep

spilled over the top of the moor, the lambs bobbing alongside like tufts of thistledown on a grey blanket. Somewhere among them were the bought and salvaged handful that were the beginning of the flock I dreamed of, the roots I longed for. I clipped the first of them at the beginning of a long day at a nearby farm and as I claimed the fine, heavy fleece I willed her to take care of herself till tupping time, and the winter dipping, and planned happily the winter's feeding that would ensure the welfare of my first crop of lambs. I was brought back to earth by a good-natured cry of 'Sheep-O'.

In recent years I have kept the job of catching the sheep in the pen where they await shearing – the catching-fold. In New Zealand where sheep are a major industry the man who takes on this task is called the Sheep-O. This information was gleaned from Godfrey Bowen, the great antipodean 'gun' shearer in his book *Wool Away*, which I bought secretly and which, when I finally and shamefacedly admitted to owning it, was borrowed and read by most of the dale. We none of us learned much about shearing from it. I am still too much of a hamfisted beginner to gain much from his methods, especially since I have never used a machine and don't particularly want to, as I long most of all to become truly proficient with hand-shears, which I carried to every clipping day like a harp to a party long before I had any sheep of my own, and the experienced shearers found that their own tried and trusted methods still worked best for them. But we learned some wonderful new words and it makes the painful, sweaty job of sheep-catching just that little bit more important when I can call myself a Sheep-O.

First the catching-fold must be filled with sheep. Enough to fill it but not to pack it so tightly that any weaklings go down and smother. I must watch at all times for fidgeting and jumping among the sheep at the back as this may mean that one is down and being stepped on by the others. This danger diminishes as the occupants are thinned out.

My two nearest neighbours usually clip together and they

will decide whose sheep are to be clipped first. They could each clip their own, but this would make things difficult for the Fleece-O's, the wives who insist on sticking meticulously to their own farm's fleeces, each clearing up after the other with a scrupulous fairness about the loose bits that makes factory demarcation look like play. This decision made, I must catch all the sheep belonging to that man, and sing out loud and clear when I have caught them all and start on the other. I must also keep my eyes open for any 'foreigners' — sheep belonging to farmers not present — as it is a shameful thing to clip a 'wrong 'un' in error.

When the shearers are ready to start, I will catch a couple of sheep, give them a shot with a dosing gun and the men will turn them up and begin. Thereafter I catch the sheep one at a time, dose them, drag them out of the pen, sit them up ready and, as each man finishes, swing the sheep into his place by the machine, take the clipped sheep from him and mark it before turning it out and slipping back into the pen to catch another.

That's it in theory, but in practice it often happens that both will finish almost together and I will have to thrust my sheep into the first pair of vacant hands and gallop back into the pen for another, swinging astride it so as to have two free hands for dosing, hoping it won't be a jumper that will bump my head on the top rail of the gate or a jibber whose trailing haunches will pull open the gate behind me and let all the others out, somehow getting it to the stand before the man bellows 'Sheep-O'.

At the end of the day my thighs will be black with bruises from the constant contact with horns, my jeans random-dyed with tar and marking fluid, my hands grey with grease and my feet whitewashed with spatters of worming mixture. As the last sheep is handed over, someone will say: 'That's the one we've been looking for all day', and I will grin. But I will be thinking secretly of the one I'm looking for. The first one to catch tomorrow.

In autumn I always itch for innovation in ways more normally associated with spring. I recall a year when my spirit of adventure called me out in the hedgerows and showed me a possibility that seemed infinitely more appealing than painting the woodwork or making curtains. Never was there such an autumn for blackberries, hips, haws, hazelnuts and the round black plums that grow almost wild in the fields round the house. The season, too, brought its quota of people who looked at all this free food in the hedgerows, pulled steadily on their metaphorical beards and foretold a hard winter.

The only hard thing fated to happen in our house was the inevitable after-effects of prolonged indulgence in over-abundant seasonal goodies which, because they are free for the taking, are eaten in unashamed excess, and not only by the children.

It was a year to encourage the grasshopper in any country dweller, and while the ant in me insisted that I should be scurrying to gather firewood, collect pine cones and cover every available surface with washed jam-jars, the very abundance of the wherewithal made nonsense of the usual urgency and tempted the idle, like myself, to frivolous pursuits. Like making wine.

For some people making wine is by no means a frivolous pursuit. There are people who drink wine regularly and enjoy it as a pleasant adjunct to good living, quite apart from those who turn the whole thing into a toppling pyramid of one-upmanship, with remarks like 'a presumptuous little wine but one cannot fail to be amused by it'. They spoil the pleasure of a simpleton like myself by offering wine and then waiting, poised, for my spoken opinion on it so they can form an unspoken one of me. It makes what may be a perfectly acceptable wine taste like the dregs in a window-cleaner's bucket and I resort to such remarks as 'I have tasted better', which is very probably true though I cannot necessarily remember the occasion and wouldn't have recognised it as a superior wine anyway.

For me, wine improves not with age but with thirst, and my pleasure in it increases in direct proportion to the acceptability of the company in which I drink it. Thus I considered myself less likely than many to be disappointed at my own efforts at winemaking.

With help from friends who had done this sort of thing before, I purchased a large plastic dustbin, put in about twenty pounds of plums, poured boiling water over them and possed them solemnly with a huge wooden spoon that my brother had carved for me out of an ash slab from the woodpile when he had been snowed in with us the previous winter, and which I had known would one day come in useful.

Andrew suggested that he would tread them for a bit to help extract the juices, but as the person who washes his socks I gave the casting vote firmly on the safe side and let him take a turn with Uncle Kevin's spoon.

After a few days I forced the resultant pulp through a colander, a teastrainer and a teatowel, then made it up with water, sugar syrup and crossed fingers to about five gallons. Then I put an improvised fermentation lock on my improvised vessel and waited for the natural yeast in the plums to send a chain of merry bubbles along the piece of plastic tubing into the jar of water, because that's what my friend Mo had said it would do.

It didn't. The liquid just lay there, smelling plummy and delicious but obviously not what you would call fermenting. A book suggested that the boiling water might have destroyed the natural yeast of the plums, so I bought some winemaking yeast from the cash chemist and made it up according to the directions so that it fizzed like brave denture cleanser before I tipped it into the must. Must, though, is simply the name for the fruit pulp basis of the wine, and not an indication of its importance. Still the liquid lay, crimson and magnificent, but I awaited the first bubble with equanimity. After all, it wasn't exactly an expensive experiment, and even if the whole process went no further and the entire vintage was consigned to the chateau lavatory to surprise the anaerobic bacteria in the septic tank with its presumption, I could always make jam again.

Nothing happened for about a week. I wondered if it was sulking. However, it seems it was simply biding its time until I was out of the way so that it could make a few tentative experiments before committing itself one way or the other.

I came home one evening after a rare excursion in adult company, together with three rather grumpy children whose bedtime had slipped by unheeded but was now sorely missed. In the middle of the kitchen floor, settling into the pattern of the new linoleum, was an ominous dark brown stain. 'Blood', said my elder son, looking accusingly at the plumpest of the cats. 'Wee', said my daughter, looking even more accusingly at the smallest. I dipped a cautious finger and sniffed, and at the same time there came from above a hiccup and a throaty gurgle, followed by another trickle of yeasty froth that splattered into the pool in front of us. 'Wine?' asked the younger lad. 'Wine,' I replied, without enthusiasm. We went upstairs and confronted the culprit.

It appeared that the container had sprung a leak somewhere because the bottle of water that was acting as a makeshift airlock was innocently half-full and the intermittent bubbles that burped into it seemed far too genteel to have caused such an overflow. So we lifted the plastic container, still inside its rigid cardboard box, and set it in the bottom of the bath below the leaky tap, to avoid further mess.

Just whose brilliant idea it was to put the plug in I have never discovered since, in the light of subsequent events, the bright spark concerned is not claiming credit and I no longer particularly want to know. But the following morning, when the pieces of disintegrated box were sliding one by one over the side of the bath, shooting the rapids caused by the steady overflow of water onto the only other piece of new linoleum in the house, I felt a definite urge to know who had boobed, and only the nagging doubt that I might have done it myself kept me from instituting a full-scale enquiry.

On examining the container it became clear that there was no leak of any kind and that the overflow had been caused by a sudden burst of activity by the hitherto dormant yeast, whose residue was now clearly seen in the bottom of the politely glugging bottle.

But glugging it was at last, and glugging it continued, safely installed in the corner of my bedroom. It was joined there by a flagon of damson which fermented agonisingly slowly, sending up one discreet bubble to every fourth one of plum's rumbling belches.

I still have a bottle or two of that wine. And it still tastes terrible.

I suppose there are many parents who find it difficult to convey to their children that there is more to Christmas than Rupert annuals and extra sweets. With the constant bombardment of advertising, the natural envy of school-fellows, the temptation of shop displays all heightened by the urgency of the season, it is hard to resist the urge to back out of the unequal struggle, to endure the sight of children at their worst, and to leave the magic out of it for fear they trample it underfoot in the rush to open their presents. Thus, when my children returned from school full of the old legend of the beasts kneeling on Christmas Eve, I was touched to hear the old story told again in their own special way, but awaited with foreboding the inevitable question – 'Is it true?'

I have very strong principles about lying to children, and therefore I did what any other parent would do in such a situation. I hedged. 'Let's wait till Christmas Eve,' I suggested, 'and then we can find out for ourselves.' I hoped fervently that they would forget.

But of course they didn't. During the evening, while we

shared the last secret preparations and set up the crib on the windowsill, one of them looked up from the task of sorting out the cows and sheep from the giraffes and bears in the animal box and asked when we were going to see if the live animals were kneeling.

It had always fascinated me, this belief that the beasts of the field do honour to the Saviour and was glad that they, too, had been captivated by it. I couldn't let them go out there and discover that this was just another story, a well-meaning embellishment to the fireside tales of Christmas. So I hedged again. I told them that it only happened at midnight, which was far too late for them to be up, and I promised that I would go and look at the proper time and tell them in the morning. They went to bed trusting me.

But what would I tell them, yes or no? I decided to say that I had been, but had been careless about the time, that I had seen nothing but that we would try again next year. I returned to the happy task of finding all the hidden hearts' desires and wrapping them up ready for morning.

But the thought stayed with me. I couldn't say that I had been if I hadn't. So somewhere between basting the slowly roasting goose and adding the last treasure to the tree, I took a torch and slipped outside for a quick peep into the fold yard. It would be all right. No lies told; no illusions shattered. I made my way round the outside of the building, listening to the heavy shuffling of the beasts within. Progress was slow as each cautious step sank into the silky mud.

The fold yard does not belong to me. It had been recently built but left incomplete and my neighbour had erected a temporary wall of wooden platforms. This, however, had left a gap at the bottom and, as any farmer will tell you, a draughty building is more injurious to livestock than no building at all, so several solid bales of bracken had been wedged in below the planks. These projected about a foot from the outside of the building. In daylight they were no hazard at all, but in darkness they were absolutely lethal. My shins met one of them with a suddenness that brought the lower half of my body to a complete standstill while the top half kept going. The torch flew out of my hand and I measured my length in the well-paddled track.

It is an entrenched belief among southerners that the people of the north adhere fervently to the maxim 'where there's muck there's brass'. As a matter of record, therefore, I point out that not a penny piece did I find as I floundered in a fair accumulation of that treasured commodity and the only jingling was the splintered ice that bobbed on the inky puddles.

I returned to the house, mission aborted. It was about half past ten.

The dog had been lying for several hours beside the cooker. I assumed that it had been simply sniffing the aroma of roast goose, Tiny Tim-style, and gave it an affectionate pat. It rose groggily and vomited prodigiously before returning to its former position. I cleaned up the mess with a wad of newspaper and took it through to burn on the sitting-room fire.

As I looked round the empty room, ready and waiting for Christmas morning, there was a sudden violent explosion and a shower of soot shot across the hearthrug. Flames roared up the chimney and the room was filled with acrid smoke. It took some minutes to realise that this was no terrorist attack but a natural consequence of earlier events. The somnolent dog had been catching drips from the oven and the contents of its stomach had been almost pure goose-fat. A Molotov cocktail could not have wreaked greater havoc among my Christmas preparations. I took mop and bucket and started again. It was almost midnight when I had finished. I felt the need of a breath of fresh air and it seemed somehow natural for me to have one last attempt at solving the kneeling question before playing Santa Claus on the way to bed.

I hadn't found my torch. I lit the old stable lamp and set forth again. I decided to leave the cattle undisturbed and visit

Bobo and Laura the goats instead. They were nearer and the way more sure.

I crossed their enclosed yard and peered into the depths of the stone building. The stable-warmth was sweet, almost tangible and I held the lamp high. The goats were chewing lazily in the far corner. Bobo, startled by the intrusion, began to rise. Slowly, stiffly, in the way of all domestic beasts, she raised her hind end, then, as she recognised me, paused, half up, half down. Kneeling.

No lightning flash, no heavenly choirs, just a little fact. Some say the creatures even speak at that special hour and old Bobo's eyes were surely telling me something then. Something I hope I shall never forget. Something I would share with the children before it was too late. She told me that this was only one of the many little miracles I had missed in my adult self-sufficiency. That the real miracles are not far away on the horizon, they are all around our feet, among the muddles, sadnesses and missed opportunities we step over every day.

I sat beside her in the straw and followed her gaze out through the doorway over the valley to the soft, dark swell of Sunburnt Nab, over whose gentle summit a single star shone very bright.

The Long Winter

The last few days of 1977 seemed destined to go down in history until the weeks, the months that succeeded them made them seem commonplace in retrospect. For over a week the weather forecasters had been suggesting tentatively that it might possibly snow in the north-east, but although we had suffered alternate bouts of coldness and wetness, never until the final Saturday had the twain met and mingled in the promised wintery showers. But when it came it came decisively, scurrying before a howling north-east wind, swirling and eddying through the chinks in the walls and fences that had the temerity to stand their ground in the face of it and whitewashing the backs of all that fled before it.

Next morning it was still snowing. Now began the miserably icy-fingered battle to feed the insistent livestock who were clearly in no mood to wait for their breakfast in such weather. The floods of the previous days were now a thick layer of ice, lying like black marzipan under the smooth snow-icing, and the doors to the yards where pig, goats and dog waited noisily were frozen immovably shut. I fetched the only implement that seemed to be of any use on these occasions — a full-sized felling axe — and hacked resolutely at the bottoms of the doors. After a while I could open all of them wide enough to squeeze through, although my early efforts cost me a duffle-coat toggle.

I went to fetch Rosalie's swill and found that I had not opened the door wide enough to admit my mum's old two-handled preserving pan in which I had boiled it. If I tipped the pan sideways the swill would all end up in my wellies and poor Rosalie was in a frenzy of anticipation. I hoisted the pan up onto the framework of the yard fence, squeezed through my hard-won entrance and then climbed up the chainlink to bring down the swill. I had a similar gymnastic tussle with the goats' water, though I was able to hurl their hay to them over the top of the wire, and I cheated by posting Ruby some strips of chop-fat through the mesh to keep her going until I felt stronger.

Of the few sheep who were lucky enough to be spending winter down by the house there was no sign. I called them and the answers came from very near. A look inside the old carthouse revealed a row of greedy, beady eyes where Snuff and the growing gimmer hoggs waited for room service.

Still it snowed; still it blew. Up onto the moor I went seeking the rest of my sheep, and found a few of them huddled dolefully under a wall with about sixty others. I fed them and went in search of the rest.

I found them half a mile away in the shelter of an untidy patch of outcrops and gullies with a hundred or so of their colleagues. I gave them what food I had been able to carry with me and went home. They were in a good place and would be safe until the wind dropped.

The next day was a carbon copy of its predecessor with the exception that one of the sheep from the first group was no longer there. Nor had she joined the second group.

Later on I went up again to where she had been the day before. I took a long stick to poke the drifts. Neighbours laughed and said I must have missed her — not recognised her all covered with snow — but I knew better. Even if I had not known her among sixty-odd sheep, she would have known me the moment I stepped through the gate, as always. In the

ace of friendly scepticism I remained convinced that Spotty
was not there.

I would not have been so worried if I had not known she
was there the day before, nor if the number present had
lessened by more than one. A sizeable group of sheep can soon
paddle themselves a clear space even in deep snow, but one on
her own is a vulnerable thing. I took a last look at the white
waste all around and went reluctantly home. Every snowdrift below the wall had been kicked apart in my fruitless
efforts.

The next day was New Year's Day. It had snowed heavily
in the night but the wicked wind had dropped and the gentle
blanket lay evenly over everything. I was up early, finished at
home by eight and up to the moor gate by ten past. My own
sheep detached themselves and floundered down to meet me.
Spotty was still not with them.

It was a crisp, still day but brilliantly sunny, and it seemed
wrong that sheep should be queueing for a handout when the
heather was showing through the snow only a couple of yards
from the gate. I kicked a path through the drift in the
gateway and sixty-some woolly bodies trooped after me and
began scratching happily for the heather they craved.

I decided to walk up a bit higher and call for Spotty. Good
old Lamb Chop trotted at my heels and I clambered up on a
hillock and hallooed as though my lungs would burst. The
sheep I had already fed jostled up for seconds but I ignored
them. From back the way I had come I heard another answering bleat.

It was Spotty. Why, when all the other sheep had crowded
below the wall, she should have chosen to stand above it, I
will never know. True, less snow was piled up against the
wall itself, but between her and the inviting heather-tips was
a great gutter, dug out in summer with a JCB then scoured
down to bedrock by the ensuing rains, and now filled with
powdery snow to a depth greater than one little Swaledale
ewe could cope with. I lay on my stomach, caught hold of her

horns and dragged her back into the safety of the flock. Then I went home for breakfast.

The snow-plough driver had just won his way through to my gate. 'Happy New Year' I cried as I sped past. Just how happy I felt at that moment he could never have guessed!

A scatter of snowflakes brushed my cheek like little friendly hands and I sang at the top of my voice the first thing that came into my head. It was one of Winnie-the-Pooh's more profound observations:

> The more it Snows (tiddley-pom)
> The more it Goes (tiddley-pom)
> The more it Goes (tiddley-pom)
> On Snowing.

It was a brute of a school holiday. It began wet and uninviting and became and remained bitterly cold. Since just after Christmas the children could spend little time outdoors without returning to the kitchen stove to whine about their chapped lips and their chilblains. The house became a glory-hole, a repository for mountains of waste paper — stories that were never completed because siblings scoffed at their beginnings and bright unfinished pictures that were not half as bad as their discouraged artists came to believe as their inexperienced fingers lagged so far behind their imaginations that even the Christmas paintboxes and fine white cartridge paper could not bolster their illusions.

Snow put an end to the twins' eagerly-awaited birthday outing before it had begun and the usual difficulties of shopping and transport made the provision of an alternative slap-up tea a bit of a damp squib.

Tempers were thin and I was tired. I was sick of coping. The leak in the pipe supplying water to the house, which had spent the summer as a fine jet, peeing gaily like that Belgian statue among the hazel bushes, had become a gurgling ributary to the adjoining stream and our water pressure had dropped alarmingly.

Nothing seemed to work any more. No doors would open or shut normally, and it seemed as though my waking hours consisted of daylong shifts of stoking fires and stomachs.

I dropped the millionth bale of hay in front for the hungry sheep and began to tease it out into manageable portions so that all the jostling queue could get a fair share. As I did so a cloud of stale fumes arose from it and I knew that I had picked a bad bale. Could I do nothing right?

Now and again I fall victim to bouts of melancholy that amount to a deep and desperate hopelessness. It seemed as though the whole world was just sitting on its fat behind waiting for me to do something or other for its comfort, and it was suddenly all too much to bear. I gathered the hay up again and climbed miserably back onto the stack to throw it over to the cattle.

I hauled two or three more bales over to the edge of the stack in an attempt to find a better sample, and one of them fell off and thudded heavily to the ground. I lifted it up and clambered wearily up alongside it.

It was then that I felt the first rough push of the wind against my shoulder. At first I saw it as just another manifestation of Sod's Law – by rights I should have been sheltered from the wind at the far end of the hayshed. Again it nudged me, rough, erratic, cheerful – warm.

And then I realised. The icy north-easter was gone and this was the longed-for deliverer, coming like young Lochinvar from out of the west, direct and strong.

You know how it is when you're feeling low. A friend's kind word of sympathy or encouragement, an offer of help with a task that seemed impossible, sometimes opens floodgates to let out all the frustration and misery in a few self-indulgent tears. The kindly touch of that strong, soft wind was enough to sit me down right there on the haybales for a good, private weep, after which I felt immeasurably better. When I climbed down the shedposts felt warm under my fingers.

The wind did not stay long, but while it was with us it worked a swift and sudden magic that turned the world green again overnight and the children spent their last day's holiday in harmony together, drawn down to the spectacular swelling of the noisy river, to the sheets of ice in the flooded meadow that were no longer too cold to handle. It did not stay long but it left a message that lightened the burden of what was to come.

The wind swung into the north-west and grew into a freezing gale; then it moved round to the north and more snow covered up all the natural conveniences once again and gave the twins another holiday after only one day back at school. But it was all made better by the memory of that brief visit and the message it left within me. Not a very original one, to be sure, but a great comfort for those who can still hear it. 'If winter comes,' it said 'can spring be far behind?'

A week later, the tender message was forgotten in another baleful blizzard. According to all the available literature on the subject, my past life ought to have been flashing before my eyes as icy hands closed once more round our neck of the woods and throttled the life out of it under cover of the year's third blanket of traffic-stopping snow.

However, since the immediate past bore such similarity to the immediate present, it seemed a waste of time to attempt to distinguish and I concentrated instead on the practicalities of the current problem.

This time we all knew it was coming, preceded by a day of tiny, splintery snow-drizzle that scattered like hundreds and thousands over the wet and heavy second snow beneath which the icy scabs of the first snow lay hidden here and there.

The next day it began in earnest, and out of the metaphorical window went Andrew's weekend parole from boarding school, and the twins, who set off up the hill with me in the very beginnings of a half-hearted wintry shower, were still shivering in their henhut refuge waiting for the school bus that had decided not to risk the journey when I crept frozen down from my daily visit to the moor sheep and we all fled home holding hands against a whirling blizzard which continued without interruption for the rest of the day.

We did a little dance in the kitchen, singing 'Hello, hello, here we are again' while the kettle boiled, and then counted the tins in the cupboard.

It continued to snow most decisively. A strike of council employees left us relatively unaffected: between the twins and the striking school meals staff was a snowdrift seven feet high which stretched for an incalculable distance. We didn't miss the snow-plough driver because his little implement would have had about as much effect as attempting to muck out a cow-byre with a teaspoon. The efforts of the brave private individual with a mechanical digger made inroads but did not achieve an outroad before the next snowfall enveloped us.

Still the twins were unable to get to school and I sought new ways of coming to terms with the situation. It has always amazed me, especially at this time of year, what some people are prepared to endure in the name of holidays.

I suppose that pictures of people wearing little and doing less in the sunspots of the world can be expected to provoke twinges of jealousy — after all, that's why the travel firms show them to us — but the thought of people spending real live money to transport themselves to places that have nothing to recommend them other than an excessive covering of snow really depresses me.

It was such lines of thought that prompted me, faced with the prospect of many days' enforced isolation in the snowy wastes, to pretend that I, too, had spent money to get here, and must fill my days with snowy pleasures whilst the chance lasted. I suggested the idea to the twins.

For the next few days they sledged on plastic bags full of hay, excavated igloos in the larger drifts, skied and skated as the fancy took them, but it was surprising how soon it palled and they returned to cradle their chilblains in front of the stove and thaw out with après-ski oxtail soup.

Is it really different if you really are on holiday? Is Swiss snow really warmer and less wet than ours, and if it isn't, then what do bona fide holiday-makers do with the steady accumulation of soggy socks and dripping jackets, the footwear coming in two by two and then sitting in grubby puddles, stuffed with newspaper and smelling indescribably foul day after interminable day before being fit for further wear?

I must admit to having had an odd whizz down the hill when no one was looking, but apart from that I found that the ordinary daily tasks expanded magically with the cold weather to fit into all the available hours of daylight with little to spare. The occasional one-off job, therefore, had to serve as a diversion.

Mending the water-pipe for instance. Now there was an optional extra for my winter break. It was becoming daily more apparent that the small round hole in the pipe supplying water to the house was becoming a larger and larger round hole. Something clearly had to be done before the pipe fractured completely and left us waterless.

At first I had lots of marvellous ideas using proprietary pipe-bodging preparations or well-advertised wonder-menders. However, such things are not to be had readily in the frozen wastes of the back of beyond and it was clear that the poor old pipe could not last out until the roads to civilisation were passable again.

So I used my initiative and the rest of the roll of aluminium foil that wrapped our Christmas dinner. I dug the pipe clear with the little brass shovel that came with the fireside companion set, and in doing so discovered that there was an even bigger hole on the underside. Obviously a case for major surgery, but I progressed with the palliative measures, fingers crossed. Over the top of the foil I squashed a piece of rubber tubing and over the top of that went yards and yards of the country person's answer to all emergencies — baler band.

The result was almost Oriental in its fiendish cunning.

Good old baler band. It really is amazing what it can be used for. Plaited and coiled it makes indestructible kitchen matting. Pulled into a more refined half-thickness, it has laced Robert's boots on many a Monday morning. It held up my waterproof over-trousers as I blundered through the snowdrifts and made natty side-reins to join Magnus' mouthing-bit to the rings on his home-made backstrap. Indoor clothes-lines and smart sheep-halters, even string bags have been created from it. We often use tight little sausages of it to liven up a fire when logs are hard to come by, and if you had walked down the hill almost any day that winter you would have seen all the doors into the enclosed yards of pig, goats and dog tied shut with familiar red and blue bows.

As the freezing weather went on and on, it became daily more difficult to attend to the needs of the housed creatures, especially Rosalie Pig, who seems to have Russian ancestry since she finds it impossible to drink out of any container without upending it when she has finished, and her door was usually frozen into the spillage. My latest device for freeing her was the insertion of the broad blade of a mattock under the door, followed by a few moments' single-minded jumping on the narrow end. This raised the door on its hinges, resulting eventually in total lift-off.

After similar performances with the other buildings, I hit upon the idea of minimising the effort by only partially shutting the doors, tying them at the tops with those dear little bows. It would not do, you see, for the goats to get out during the night, because if they did the ducks who share their accommodation would also be let loose and then I should, in all probability, never see them alive again. For the Red Baron was back.

Not long before, my neighbour lost all his handful of old faithful hens to the neighbourhood fox, and since that day the four-footed fiend had turned his attentions to the Drysdale homestead. Each day's fresh cover of snow had been imprinted with his neat, pointed dog-feet, joined by the narrow brushmark of his sweeping tail.

People in other lands tell of mysterious tracks made by fabulous monsters – the Yeti and the Sasquatch. I think I'd rather be visited by something legendary than by this readily identifiable, everyday hooligan whose visits always end, sooner or later, in grief and loss.

So in with the goats each night went Mildred, Onion and the rest, since they can't roost high with the hens and won't stay sheltered with the sheep. And there each morning were the tracks, circling the house and coming nightly nearer, ever nearer. I grassed to the gamekeeper, but he already knew.

One morning, on my way to the postbox, I caught sight of him, whisking through the trees. He was not slinking as I always expect foxes to do, but stepping out gaily in search of easy pickings. I stopped at once, but he had heard me. For a moment our eyes met and then he was gone like the swirl of a red silk scarf among the alders.

I felt vaguely uncomfortable, slightly annoyed. How much easier it would be to hate him if he were not so very, very beautiful.

In early February there came a single, beautiful day. There was still snow, but not quite everywhere, and in the spaces where it had been things were coming to life again. Here and there in the middle of the meadows, molehills popped through the white crust like gravy boiling out of a shepherd's pie, and bare ground showed through again in one or two favoured spots around the house. At the foot of the old pine tree the little hollows where the hens loved to scratch were free at last, and on this morning every last one of them lay sprawled in the blessed sunshine, legs and wings stuck out at crazy angles like participants in an orgy, which in a way they were, bless them, celebrating in their own way the return of life as they know and enjoy it to their own particular territory which had been hungry and joyless for so long. Perhaps they were celebrating a little in advance of the event, but that morning I couldn't blame them, for I, too, felt that surge of gaiety that the sunshine brought with it, and even though there was not enough heat in it to thaw any more of the lying snow, it is always pleasant to see a long-absent friend.

Rhoda the cockerel felt called upon, for the first time in his young life, to single out one or two of the more responsive hens for an impressive display of masculinity, rising at last above the rather ridiculous name we gave him when we thought he was a pullet. Round and round he strutted, trailing one wing and fluttering his black and white neck-feathers like a Fulham supporter's scarf.

On the very top of the hill above the house, green grass was showing, and Magnus the pony flung himself joyfully on it, rolling crazily and finally hauling himself to his feet with a cry of 'wheeeeee!' and careering wildly downhill again with his hind feet, for the greater part of the time, waving higher than his head.

Sheep fled in all directions so that I was forced to put him into his loosebox until after they had finished their breakfast, when he continued his dramatic dancing display, rolling in a pool of sunshine that turned his straw bedding to old gold before his sparkling eyes.

The sheep on the moor were digging busily, extending the area of the excavations to uncover the buried heather yet again and the goats, growing daily heavier with their living cargo, spread themselves outdoors in the sun.

All the creatures with whom we share our lives here seemed to be gathered together to celebrate the return of the sunshine, to make the most of this brief appearance, this earnest of good faith, this promise of the re-awakening still to come and not, after all, so very far away.

By the end of the month, though, we were snowed in yet again, this time for longer than ever. The editor of the local paper had difficulty in deciphering one week's column. This was because it was, in fact, the previous week's column and had lain for seven long days in a mucky puddle in the little letterbox at the end of our lane, cut off from the rest of the world which, in turn, didn't seem in too much of a hurry to reach us.

On the day the postman finally managed to empty the box, I waylaid him along a farm lane. There he sat in his Land-rover, with his flask and his sandwiches, drying off the soggy letters as best he could. It was the first in a long series of rescue operations which began that day and continued, with varying degrees of success, up till the next let-up in the bad weather which came just in time to save the last few days of Andrew's half-term holiday, but too late to save poor Nancy's school trip to London, in which she had invested every penny of her potato-picking money.

I had to make the decision on the day as to whether she could walk the six miles to school to join them. Necessity had forced me to blunder to the nearest farm and to flounder out on to the moor, and some of the drifts would have been head-high on a child. I decided that it was an unreasonable risk and she stayed at home. She did not grumble once, and I felt very small when I considered the amount of moaning I'd been doing over the previous fortnight.

The week's enforced absence gave way to the official half-term holiday, and the twins sledged frequently and wetly. The house was full of little dark, damp piles, which proved to be nothing more sinister than discarded socks and damp drawers but which none the less gave one a bit of a turn when trodden on in the dingy early-morning grope across the living-room to put back the only functioning light-bulb after its regular tour of duty upstairs overnight.

I have no idea what causes these occasional outbursts of unrest among my bulbs, but they show commendable solidarity — one out, all out. On this occasion perhaps they came out in sympathy with the plumbing.

This too had suffered a seasonable disability which manifested itself first in a reluctance of the bathwater to quit the house by the usual channels and a great shower of lovely icicles which hid the downpipe for days.

This I could live with, but before long other signs of effluent unease became apparent. Using the lavatory ceased to be a relief and became more of an investment; each time we flushed it we got back more than we put in.

Thus I spent the first of March's few fine days emptying the septic tank — a lonely job — with the help of all the special-ised equipment at my disposal — a bucket tied on to a bit of rope and a long stick with which to submerge it.

One thing that can be said for snow is that it covers things. Obvious, perhaps, but when it goes there gradually appears a week's work where it has been and you suddenly realise that it has been acting like a freshly-laundered cloth on a scratched table. Under the snow, who's to say our garden isn't as perfect as anyone else's? But as it receded like an ebbing tide it left a pile of debris that made tidying the yard more like beach-combing. Here and there appeared flower pots, trowels, rubber balls and bits of string that had been left lying and snowed upon, and all those sheep who came down from the moor to shelter from the great blizzard left a surprising amount of evidence of their visit.

So it was shovel and soapsuds time again and the sunshine, for the moment, beckoned. I wondered if this time we had seen the last of winter.

One item we found was the lid of the dustbin. Long weeks ago, before I filled the peggy-tub with stones and set it behind the gate to withstand her onslaughts, Rosalie Pig had burst into the yard and shouldered the bin over to root among its contents. She didn't stay for long because anything re-motely edible had always been incorporated into her swill, but before I had discovered her at her mischief one of the north-easterly gusts had caught up the lid and tossed it like a mighty frisbee to somewhere just out of sight. Then it snowed.

Now a dustbin without a lid is no dustbin at all — more like an unwieldy bucket — so throughout the long white winter we used it as a firewood container. There wasn't much point in having a dustbin anyway as the snow had closed the road down to the house since Christmas and no one came to empty it, so we stored all the rubbish in sacks to wait, like everything else, for the better weather.

Then one day Robert strode into the yard bearing the lost lid like a shield before him and it was clear that, industrial disputes permitting, we should be seeing the binmen that week. I was tired and cross after a day's grudging domesticity and I felt quite unreasonably disappointed that the first real sign of the approach of spring should be the reappearance not of the snowdrops, but of the dustbin lid.

When I took the dog out later that evening, she found another treasure. The roaring of the river at the bottom of the hill drew us down to view its temporary magnificence and there beside the brown turbulence, curled up small, lay a Leeds United supporter's scarf. It belonged to Andrew and must have been left down there during the Christmas holidays. I brought it home again.

March. Surely there should be something by now? One of nature's perennial signs to cheer the last few days before the official start of spring. Nothing. We'd had the odd fine day, breaking up the winter into deep frozen-portions, and I'd relished them, but now I felt the need of a token of good faith from somewhere outside these sodden surroundings, and I could not find it.

I went up to the moor as always to call my sheep for their handful of extra food. Most of the snow had gone, even where the great drifts lay piled behind the walls. I fed the familiar faces and wandered up to have a look.

Morbidly, I walked the length of the stone wall, fingers crossed, looking for sheep that may have lain beneath the snow. I saw one, ran to her, recognised her, and stood gazing down. It was the creeper. A poor little sheep, not one of mine, old and frail, she had fumbled her way back and forward along the wall and I had known that her days were numbered long before the snow came. She lay neatly in an attitude of sleep, her head on her flank, just as the snow had enveloped her. Poor little creeper. I would miss her doddering figure, but hers was the only carcase and for that I was grateful.

I looked all around me and there was nothing unusual to see. In the middle distance a tiny patch of snow in a vast expanse of dark heather. The last little patch of clean white snow. I set off to walk towards it.

But it wasn't snow. It was a huge seagull, limp, dead. It was on its back with its head bent under it, ugly and undignified, with only the breathtaking whiteness of its underparts left to hint at the former beauty of it. I picked it up and held the heavy head with its great cruel beak splashed with scarlet, fascinated by the sightless eyes.

I smoothed the soft grey wings into place beside the body and laid it down again in the heather in as near as I could manage to an attitude of peace.

From nowhere another bird rose above me, its silhouette clumsy against the clear sky, emphasising the grace of its fallen cousin. This bird was dark and graceless in its flight, its wings blunt, its tail awkward. When it spoke its voice was unbeautiful.

But by its voice I knew it. A lapwing. The first of the year. And if the voice was ugly, its message was sweet indeed. It spoke, at last, of spring.

But it lied. As March ended, winter it seemed was only just getting into its stride.

It was just before five. To find that out I had to raise the alarm clock from its prone position – arise, Sir Clock – and peer into its honest face.

According to the guarantee, which has always lain across its feet in the place a female penguin carries her egg, I've had it since 1972. That guarantee has long since expired, but the old clock has given faithful service since my Mum collected it from the Green Shield gift shop in Chelmsford all those years ago. It still keeps perfect time and never forgets to ring, provided I never forget to let it lie on its face overnight. I feel it has earned that privilege – after all, I don't fancy the idea of spending the night standing up myself.

Nor, incidentally, did I relish the idea now, but it must be done. I began to grope for clothes. Normally these would have lain across the bottom of the bed, keeping warm, but last night I received a visit from a strange white-and-tabby tomcat who picked a fight with one of our cats in the corner of my bedroom, and what was not scattered by my disorderly arousal was thrown at the departing marauder. Slowly I began.

Over the most basic of essentials went a cotton shirt and a pair of thick wool tights, then two woollen jerseys. Next, thigh-length seaboot stockings, foam rubber welly-liners, Levis, ancient sheepskin jacket, gloves from the oven and wellies from the pool of water inside the kitchen door. This brought me to the threshold; a quick lift of the latch and I was out into the black and white world that has no business to be outside my door at this time of year. Going to the barn, ice cracking under my feet in the depressing darkness of our own collective making – why do we still fiddle with the clocks twice a year? – and savouring the little thrill of pleasure that filled the moment before I inserted a gloved finger into the latch-hole and opened the door to see if Snufkin had arrived.

For, whatever the weather, it was time. The first of our lambs was soon to embark on the first of its hazards and it looked like being a mean and inhospitable welcome for the poor mite. I had already been out late the previous night and perhaps I could have had another hour in bed, but with the grim practicality that this sort of weather encouraged, I liked to see what might have happened before the daily 'lamb bank' announcement on the radio. After all, however much we longed for Snufkin, as we had already named it, to come and cheer us all, old Snuff must want it more and if she were to have a tragedy, as she did once before, I would have to find a foster lamb for the old girl somehow.

I wished they had got the road open. There was still an awful lot of snow between us and civilisation. I had a vague plan half formed that I might be able to walk into Osmotherly with a rucksack and pick up a lamb there — after all I walked almost that far last year to collect one for Lamb Chop.

Lamb Chop. With the thought came the reality. As I closed the barn door on old Snuff, still alone, there appeared at my heels that squat little Swaledale sheep with the fly-away horns and behind her Sparrow, Ugly, Georgina and the others, all well on in lamb themselves, and enjoying their unseasonal holiday down-country, enforced by the violence of the storm that had only now abated into freezing tranquillity. I had no intention of feeding them before their usual time, but I took off one glove and pulled a few ears and stroked a few noses before I scuttled into the house again to make my first blessed mug of tea, and as I supped gratefully at the bubbles round the rim of my fine new enamel mug, I rejoiced that our small flock of moor sheep were all down, all safe, all accounted for.

It had begun on Friday, when the school taxi did not come for the twins, and Lamb Chop did not turn up at feeding time. I worried. It was the first time she had ever missed the daily hand-out and I could only assume that the mounting violence of the wind had driven her into shelter somewhere. We had an early lunch and then I set off to look for her. First to a neighbour, to see if she had turned up among his ewes, and I traded information (negative) for my assistance with the shifting of a cow and calf, then up onto the moor to circle the lower running and search all the sheltered places where she might be, finding in the process, I hoped, any of anyone else's sheep unwisely placed.

Sheep, especially when getting heavy in lamb, often run

before a storm, so I'm told, and it seemed a good idea to visit all the wall-backs and gravelly gutters I could reach in an afternoon. There were a few ewes under the wall above the road but they were being fed daily by my neighbour and were better off where he could reach them easily. I followed the wall up as far as the old village school and was glad I had done so. The narrow track was filling in fast with snow, and any ewe caught there wouldn't stand a chance. At least I could say for certain that no sheep had been there.

I finished a little way up Cow Rigg, on my knees, facing into the wildest blizzard I have ever known, with my face stiff and aching, unable to open my eyes because of the spikelets of ice in the tearing wind – I knew it was time to go home, so I groped my way to my last wall and followed it back to the moor end, driving ahead of me the three sheep I had found there. Lamb Chop was waiting for me in the intake when I got back, but the ration of ewe cobs I had carried for her in my pocket were too wet to eat, and I threw them away.

The following morning the blizzard howled on unabated. I went up to feed my sheep, knowing that they had all been present the night before, calling and encouraging them to come to me. I heard a few answering bleats, so I went on up to the top wall, calling as I went into the teeth of the icy wind.

Dear God, what a sight! Snow, piled in great floundering heaps under the wall and among it the sheep, almost unrecognisable as living creatures. Some were standing below the drifts, moving as they grew, almost indistinguishable from their surroundings. Some were on top of the drifts, standing higher than the wall where they had paddled round and round to keep the ground solid beneath their feet, and here and there were the heads of those who had stopped moving and let the quiet killer swirl round their necks, content to wait, to die. Worst of all were the sheep who had lain down within the groups of trampling sheep; it was to these – or at least to those I could see – that I turned first. It took all my strength to pull them to their feet, and great handfuls of wool were torn out in the process. They were frozen to the ground. It was not yet eight o'clock.

Clearly I would have to get all the sheep away from that wall at least once. Even if they went back again, they wouldn't be buried before the other sheep's owners could come and shift them all again. I shouldered my way into the first drift, caught one of my own sheep by the horn and pulled her down to ground level; the others followed her, floundering down the track I had made. I could see three more heads, so fearing that these might be as severely frozen-down as the first ones I had rescued, I went to the nearest house to borrow a spade. By the time I got back with it I could hardly see them. In all I found only seven, but only the thaw would tell me for sure how many there really were.

None of mine had been in serious difficulties. The handful of cake they had been getting as their lambs grew heavier had made a difference that showed on that frightful morning. Concentrate rations are not normally fed to moor sheep, and many of them, though not our local ones, I'm proud to say, only see hay in a crisis. But our own few sheep are all that we have and my reasoning is that cobs in the ewe-bank would do us more good than pennies in the piggy-bank when lambing-time came and we counted our dividends. This wicked winter justified my extravagance.

I had not the authority nor the ability to take all these sheep to the in-bye, but at least I could make that job easier. I used my own sheep to work a track down to the gate, and it was down that track that they all came, later in the day, to stay in safety till the worst had passed.

I finished my tea and made another cup. I settled down by one bar of the electric fire to dream about Snufkin. In Tove Jansson's Moomin books, Snufkin is a wandering little character whose visits are welcomed by the Moomin-trolls because his coming means the end of the long winters. So would our Snufkin bless it, when it came.

One of the local farmers said to me, 'Cheer up, Missus,

Spring is just around the corner.' 'Which corner? I'll go and meet it,' I said.

I was tired, tired of winter and tired, too, of spring in the way that one tires of an awaited friend whose coming is delayed and the possibilities of the visit staled by conjecture so that their eventual arrival is a muddled let-down.

In a few days time, I would be thirty-seven. This depressed me, because I was only expecting to be thirty-six, arithmetic being one of my shakier capabilities. I couldn't escape the feeling that someone had stolen a year from me, wasted and hidden it somehow in the long, cold gap between Christmas and Easter.

Little things suddenly caused me annoyance out of all proportion to their gravity. Pootle the kitten was taken short on the quarry tiles in the corner of the sitting room. The lapse itself wasn't especially disastrous, but the ensuing mime, the exaggerated pretence of covering the evidence, suddenly appeared as an insult to my intelligence and I threw a Beano annual at him. What was happening to me?

I can remember longing for signs of spring, sure that everything would be all right when the crocuses came by the telephone box, when the snowdrops showed through, when the lapwings came, the chicks were due, when Snufkin arrived.

The crocuses, as they came, were chewed off at ground level by ravenous sheep and the snowdrops under my neighbour's wall were trampled and filthied by the poor bedraggled hens that could find no shelter anywhere else. The lapwings stood mournfully up to their knackety back-to-front knees in the brown water that ran down their nesting fields, and I dreaded the arrival of the first chicks because, unless things improved, they would drown and die in the ubiquitous soul-swallowing mud.

Can you believe that one day I had to rescue a duck that had given up the unequal struggle against the slow black tide? That must be what it's like to be trapped in an oil slick.

None of the farmers round here could remember a worse winter and still it showed no signs of leaving. Its fury subsided now and again to petulance, but it would not go and I was tired. Tired of what it had done to my small dreams of a better life, a gentler way. Tired of seeing the fantasy I wove round our isolation and poverty lifted like a torn tarpaulin to expose the parts I had tried so successfully to hide, to ignore.

When Snufkin finally came, lifting her lovely salt-and-pepper face to the sprinkling of snow that touched her even before her mother's warm tongue, there lay beside her a small dead brother and the culmination of long weeks of waiting was somehow spoiled by what might have been. I told myself that I was greedy and that made me even more miserable because I knew it was true. If ever my resolve was tested, that winter stretched it thinner than ever before; almost to breaking point. But not quite.

In a friend's house, I saw their daughter, struggling with a dropped stitch, throw her knitting at her mother without a word, confident that she would sort out the problem and hand it back so that she would be able to carry on. I think I wanted to drop the whole worrying muddle our life here had become onto someone's lap, just as she did, and have it all sorted out and handed back to me, fresh and ready to start again.

The next Wednesday, at about four o'clock, it started to snow. Again. Wet, heavy, slapping my face like clammy hands. I worried. A local man, not given to panic, once told me of a spring snowstorm that killed a lot of sheep in these parts. The wind freshened, the snow flopped thicker. It seemed impossible that such weighty stuff could drift, but it was drifting, sure enough. I had never seen such extraordinary snow and it frightened me. I snapped at the children. When Nancy asked why, I told her I was worried about the sheep on the moor. 'Go up and get them,' she said.

What a daft idea. When the first snow came, before Christmas, a gruff neighbour asked where my sheep were, and when I said they were out among the heather he humphed and said he had expected them to be at home by the fire. I felt ashamed of the thought. I walked up to the moor gate. Great gouts of wet snow fell from the overhanging trees and it was as though someone was throwing wet dishcloths. I walked like a clockwork thing up into the driving snow. When I was far enough away so that no one human could hear me, I called my sheep and from under the wall almost all of them detached themselves and came to me, trustingly. I called again. From one of the week-old drifts by the wall a sheep called. It proved to be a very old greyfaced ewe who often ate with mine because I felt her boldness and persistence had earned her that privilege. I had decided to take my sheep down the moor and put them into the barn where Snuff and Snufkin sheltered already. Even from where I stood I could see the bodies of the two sheep I had missed in the earlier rescue. It sickened me to realise that I had been standing on their poor buried heads when I was digging out their more fortunate companions and their hopeless faces haunted me daily. I began to walk down, and my sheep came beside me, but the old ewe by the wall still called to me. 'You can come too,' I told her, but she didn't move, just called again. I went to her.

There in the snow at her feet, already half-covered with icy whiteness, lay a lamb. My shoulders ached with the weight of my sodden coat and there was no time for ceremony. I was still a sheep short, but all the heaviest in lamb were with me. Sparrow would have to take her chance with the others left out. I lifted the lamb in the crook of my left arm, hauled the old ewe by the horn with my right and we all set off, my own sheep jostling and bumping and threatening to knock me down. At the gate I left the ewe and lamb to mother-up and led my cheerful flock down to the barn, still feeling guilty at this panic action. I went for the sheep and lamb. The lamb could not stand, the ewe would not. I went back home again, intending to get a fertiliser bag to sledge them down. I told

Nancy where I was going. 'Can I help?' she asked.

Could she? Was it not wickedness to take a child out in such conditions? Of course it was but, looking at it another way, was it not equally wrong to deny a willing child the chance of the sort of satisfaction that such an adventure might bring? 'Do you really want to?' I asked, but she did not answer because she was groping under the couch for her wellingtons.

So down we came, Nancy carrying the precious little scrap of life. I carried the ewe, who seemed to have given up hope. In the Dutch barn we built a shelter of straw bales and left the pair there to recover.

Two hours later we were outside again with the ewe sat up like a kangaroo and the lamb sucking at the first vital drops. We had done all we could.

Suddenly the whole place was alive with sheep and there among them was Sparrow. I had not been the only one to fear the storm, and the confirmation of the rightness of my decision was the fact that my neighbour had done the same thing. He had brought Sparrow. I had brought the old grey-faced ewe. A life for a life. Self-sufficiency is an impossible aim for such as myself, but inter-dependence has its satisfactions too.

Later that night the long power-cut began; the following morning the dramatic flood swept through the house, but between those two was a blessed, tiny breathing space in which we sat in candlelight eating sandwiches. Robert noticed that Nancy's leg was bleeding where her wellington had cut through the skin. 'I know,' she told him, 'but it was worth it.' I saw the glow in her eyes and knew that here, suddenly, was one child to whom I would never have to explain why I chose this crazy life. Perhaps one day she will even explain it to me.

The paper aeroplane whizzed past my cheek and landed on the draining board. I picked it up and skimmed it out over the lower half of the kitchen door and it scattered a collection of somnolent ducks before embedding itself nose first in the woodpile.

Andrew went out to retrieve it and it soared in again, narrowly missing a row of bottles on the windowsill. His grinning face appeared over the door and I held up the offending aircraft menacingly pointed in his direction. 'Steady with that, Mum,' he said. 'It took me a whole month to make it!'

I looked at the folded paper, which I knew very well to have been no more than the work of the last few idle minutes, and noticed that it was made from a torn-off page from the kitchen calender. A whole month indeed! I threw it at him. All the same, it was something of a surprise to realise that May really had gone. Good riddance.

A week or so earlier I had met an acquaintance in Northallerton mart who asked me how I had survived the winter. I told him that I would tell him when it was over and we both laughed, but I wasn't entirely joking. Even as May drew to a close, this long and fearful winter was still with us, still taking its punishing toll. May was as cold, hopeless and spiteful as the months that preceded it, and as it left it thumbed its nose at us in the worst way it could find.

On the first of May Nancy had danced like a dervish among whirling snowflakes, saying they reminded her of the locusts in the Bible, but on its final day we had the heaviest rainfall I can remember since coming to the house, and we battled for over an hour with flash flooding of frightening severity. The land around us had been waterlogged for weeks. There was just no room for the sudden heavy rainfall and a great sheet of water swept down the hill above the house and swirled through the yard. Rosalie Pig's sty was hock-deep and little Cally the baby goat had to be carried to safety as her house was flooded from a cascade that smashed her roof and a tidal wave that swept in through the door. In bludgeoning a track through the middle for the water to run away I managed to drown two of Onion's precious ducklings who were shelter-ing beyond it. The children and I worked till dark to mop up.

In the yard, behind the old stone trough, the water had found a new route into the stone drain below. Nancy shrieked that she had found a Wirzel-hole and we ran to look. The water was swirling in a brown bubbling whirlpool, round and round like a giant's dirty bathwater and the noise of it was lost in the general roar so that it appeared to be sucked silently down to the nether regions. We watched, fascinated, until Robert broke the spell.

'If we were in Australia,' he said, 'that water would be going round the other way.'

I looked around us at the slackening storm, the sand strewn over everything, the broken branches, and the acres and acres of cold, wet weather and said with feeling: 'Would that we were, lad, would that we were.'

It was June before we got straight again.

Epilogue

A great deal has happened since we came to Hagg House. I have learned a lot about moorland life and about myself. I have started to build a flock of sheep. I have almost written a book. How nice to end it Happy-ever-after; but that would be dangerous until I am more certain that it will be so.

In the days when I worked in London on a monthly magazine, a favourite cautionary tale among the senior staff was that of an article in a rival publication which had begun: 'Princess Margaret has proved surprisingly adaptable as a young wife and mother . . .' In the normal process of circulation copies were sent up to Scotland in advance of the publication date — and went on sale a day or two before the birth of Her Royal Highness's first baby.

In a similar spirit of misguided topicality I once wrote the opening paragraphs of a newspaper column before the arrival of one of the chief protagonists and scrapped them hurriedly in the face of the stark realities with which I was confronted when he made his appearance.

This was to be the idyll at last entered upon by poor Dodo, the lone guinea-fowl whose sex I had been at such pains to determine. While I arranged delivery of the long-awaited mate I planned the writing of my story. 'Once upon a time . . .' it began.

I had asked every friend, acquaintance and passer-by that

might solve the mystery of the unhappy little vulture to which I had fallen heir some weeks previously. I was told, tongue-in-cheek, to shake it and see if it rattled and once, just in case, I tried it, furtively. The poor Dodo was at once overcome by one of its hysterical turns and drowned any faint rattle with its dolorous shrieks. I couldn't really blame it, but nor could I help wishing that it would exhibit just a shred of co-operation in my efforts to determine the one basic necessity for its physical and emotional fulfilment. Equality of opportunity is a laudable standpoint but there are some functions that demand a degree of discrimination. I decided that as soon as I received three educated guesses in either direction I would purchase another bird of opposite inclination, but even my most knowledgeable associates seemed unwilling to commit themselves.

Finally, however, a friend declared, with some authority, that the mis-shapen fowl mumping apologetically after its bantam foster mother was more than likely female, and I congratulated him on being the third man of that persuasion and ordered a cock bird without further delay.

I collected Archie from a friend's back-door handle, where he swung giddily in a hessian sack. I didn't dare examine him for fear of a break for freedom so, trusting the vendor and assuming that it is only pigs that should not be bought in pokes, I took him home. At the top of the hill I laid the sack down to see if there was any post for me and, feeling his feet on the ground, the invisible occupant began to gallop downhill under his own steam. As I watched, the sack gathered speed and I had to put on quite a spurt to overtake it before it left the road and struck off across country. The poor fellow had been in the sack since first light and had missed breakfast and lunch. It seemed only fair to ensure him a bite of supper.

I shut the door into the poultry's yard and let him gently out of the sack. I attached a long piece of string to one leg, like a wary falconer, and stepped back as I tossed a handful of corn at him. This proved to be a big mistake as he interpreted it as an act of aggression and flew up with an aggrieved shriek over the top of the wire fence and into a large plum tree. The string slipped like parboiled spaghetti through my helpless fingers and hung tantalisingly just out of reach.

Then began one of the chases that have become a recurring feature of my stock-keeping ventures. A quick poke with a thumb-stick brought the truant down to the ground and he scampered, grumbling, hither and yon while I made occasional fruitless lunges for the end of the string. I made a cup of strong coffee and tore up the few sugary paragraphs that I had already written.

When I came out I saw an opportunity, grabbed, held tight, and then found that I had seized the poor Dodo who had hitherto shown no interest in her chosen mate.

The effect on Archie was, however, electric. Hearing the cries of distress he rallied to her assistance and was immediately set upon by the bantam cockerel. He retired, *hors de combat*, to the plum tree.

As dusk fell, all the poultry returned to their sleeping quarters but Archie, stubborn to the last, flew up onto the roof and walked up and down the ridge tiles, his nails clicking rhythmically while the last of the light faded and I gave up and went indoors.

In the morning the pair of them had got together but were both following the little bantam with the same do-or-die air. I noticed with a sinking feeling that they were very alike and that Archie had lost his identifying string. Only Dodo's raucous 'Come back, come back' and Archie's intermittent 'Oi!' provided definite distinction and even then it was difficult to tell which was saying which at any given time. But the pair of them took to withdrawing to the top of the haystack for private, creaking conversations and I took that to be a good sign.

Convention clearly decreed that I should claim that they will live happily ever after, and so it has proved until now, but in their immediate and limited world security is hard to maintain and tragedy can be swift and final. They are happy, let us say, for the present.

So many changes have taken place here since I came looking for something and began my struggle to make it real. The fight to keep it will be harder still and in quiet moments I face the fact that the cause is perhaps already lost.

Once I heard a local farmer tell an efficiency expert that his farm was more than his business, it was a way of life. I knew then that this was what I wanted for myself and the children. But since those days rents in the dale have gone from peppercorns to pounds of flesh and the carrying of passengers is uneconomic and therefore unpopular. The dale is passing into the hands of the new, the young, the go-ahead. But what is it that lies ahead? One day I took time to ponder on it.

The ground under the scattered hay was warm, but wet from the rain of the day before.

After over a week of uninterrupted haymaking, we had been forced to take a break. All the bales were stacked. In the newly shaven field above the house the light breeze had dried the ground so that it was quite fit to sit on, and I sat on it, watching the goats pick their way up the sides of the road. There wasn't so much for them to clean up as there had been in other years, because of the new grass cutter, which can get nearer to the edges than the old one.

The herbage at the edge of the field used to be quite different in character from the rest – a special accumulation of knapweed and moondaisies, crowding together as though they knew this part of the meadow was safe from the knife, and in the top corner, too steep for the old finger-bar mower, the gorgeous harebells, too delicate to survive the rigours of drastic regeneration, have been encroached upon. I used to love that little corner of the field. It reminded me of one of the favourite poems of my childhood – 'Where the thistle lifts a purple crown, Six foot out of the turf, And the harebell shakes on the windy hill . . .'

Admittedly, the poem is about Sussex, but some things do overlap into these northern hills. Or did.

I love to hear the local folk reminisce about the way things were done in the old days. All the same a little shiver ran down my back as I thought about how much change has come about in the ten years since I came here. I lay back on the whiskery ground and remembered what I have almost come to look upon as 'old times'. I thought about the implements that have arrived, one-by-one on the neighbouring farms. The muckloader, which replaced the good old handfork within the span of my memory. The fine new hayscattering things which everybody seems to have invested in. All of them replacing people, doing jobs that I could have done if only I had arrived in time. Replacing me. It is by doing jobs – not for money, for the Trades Unions have made it so that nobody can afford to employ me, and so that by exercising the basic human right of putting my own price on my own labour I place any employer in jeopardy, but for payment in kind – that I manage to run this little holding. If I stack bales throughout haytime, I earn hay for the creatures. If I work hard on clipping days I earn the chance for my own sheep to get dosed with the more expensive anthelmintics that are only marketed in containers sufficient for a hundred or more ewes. If I pick potatoes, I get potatoes for the winter and if I hoe turnips, I get a few for the pot. It seems so logical. I don't really aspire to owning money, although I appreciate the wisdom of saving for rainy days. But does it have to be money?

What little I make is invested all right – invested in the livestock, roaming the moors and appreciating steadily. I see my savings grow not on slips of paper from a stockbroker, but making themselves over again in miniature on cold, spring mornings and I count my hoard, such as it is, into safety in winter storms. I suppose, being a simple soul, I find the mechanics of sexual reproduction easier to grasp than the workings of compound interest. To each, I suppose, his own.

My point of view, though, used to be a very common one. In the good old days.

I wanted, in a vague way, to become a farmer, because it seemed a way of life that was geared to community, to working together, to sharing basic tasks, but it isn't like that any more. I am witnessing the passing of the way of life I have fought so hard to attain.

More and more, the mechanised aids to farming are geared to one-man operation, and the farmer will soon be one of the loneliest men on earth. It brings a whole new meaning to self-sufficiency and it depresses me. There are so few jobs left to the willing labourer. My neighbours can manage perfectly well without me, but not I without them. I am being left behind.

This year the turnips were put in with a precision drill and another of my potential contributions is rendered valueless. Across the river, another farmer is trying out a new flat-eight bale stacking system, and, to my misery, it seems to be working very well. How long, I wonder, before one of those moves in next door.

One, two, three fields from where I sit, an ancient hay-making implement serves as a makeshift gate. There it sits, all overgrown and taken for granted. Nobody remembers it, other than as something to turn cattle. I expect I shall end up like that, phased out and forgotten. Will anyone remember what I was for?

I rose stiffly and went back to the house. I dug a grave for the little Maran hen who tried to defend her brand-new chickens from sudden danger in the only way she knew how. The skin was flayed from her back by the whirling blades of the brand-new grasscutter. 'I've never cut grass so fast,' said the driver, happily. I buried her beside the two ducklings who couldn't run quite fast enough the day before. I didn't complain, because it was too late and they were, technically, trespassing but most of all because I didn't want to hear anyone suggest that they were expendable. Not to me they weren't.

I thought of an epitaph for them — 'They paid the price of progress' — and I stood and wondered. I suppose the price of progress is just another sort of tax, like VAT and we must all pay at the going rate, pay up and look happy.

I shall pay if I must — but look happy? Never!

Another dalesman once told two feuding neighbours to go and climb the hill that lay opposite them and look over the top at a whole new world. My beloved home is being swept up that hill on the tide of progress and soon we will all be able to see what lies beyond it.

But I came from the other side of that hill, and I could tell them if they would only listen. It is something grander than Hawnby; something greater than Helmsley. It is Hull. It is Halifax. It is Hell.